MINUTE GUIDE TO

OUTLOOK™ 97

by Sue Plumley

A Division of Macmillan Computer Publishing
201 West 103rd St., Indianapolis, Indiana 46290 USA

To all of the diligent people at Que whose hard work, great ideas, and friendliness contributed to this book and others I've written for them.

©1997 Que Corporation

Library of Congress Catalog Card Number: 96-70774

International Standard Book Number: 0-7897-1018-8

99 98 97   8 7 6 5 4 3 2 1

Interpretation of the printing code: the rightmost double-digit number is the year of the book's first printing; the rightmost single-digit number is the number of the book's printing. For example, a printing code of 97-1 shows that this copy of the book was printed during the first printing of the book in 1997.

Screen reproductions in this book were created using Collage Plus from Inner Media, Inc., Hollis, NH.

Printed in the United States of America

Publisher   Roland Elgey

Publishing Manager   Lynn E. Zingraf

Editorial Services Director   Elizabeth Keaffaber

Managing Editor   Michael Cunningham

Director of Marketing   Lynn E. Zingraf

Acquisitions Editor   Martha O'Sullivan

Technical Specialist   Nadeem Muhammed

Product Development Specialist   Faithe Wempen

Technical Editor   Herb Feltner

Production Editor   Audra Gable

Book Designer   Glenn Larsen

Cover Designer   Dan Armstrong

Production Team   Angela Calvert, Kim Cofer, Tricia Flodder, Maureen Hanrahan, Janelle Herber, Christopher Morris, Gina Rexrode, Megan Wade

Indexer   Sandra Henselmeier

We'd Like to Hear from You!

As part of our continuing effort to produce books of the highest possible quality, Que would like to hear your comments. To stay competitive, we *really* want you, as a computer book reader and user, to let us know what you like or dislike most about this book or other Que products.

You can mail comments, ideas, or suggestions for improving future editions to the address below, or send us a fax at (317) 581-4663. For the online inclined, Macmillan Computer Publishing has a forum on CompuServe (type **GO QUEBOOKS** at any prompt) through which our staff and authors are available for questions and comments. The address of our Internet site is **http://www.mcp.com/que** (World Wide Web).

In addition to exploring our forum, please feel free to contact me personally to discuss your opinions of this book: I'm **75703,3251** on CompuServe, and I'm **lgentry@que.mcp.com** on the Internet.

Although we cannot provide general technical support, we're happy to help you resolve problems you encounter related to our books, disks, or other products. If you need such assistance, please contact our Tech Support department at 800-545-5914 ext. 3833.

To order other Que or Macmillan Computer Publishing books or products, please call our Customer Service department at 800-835-3202 ext. 666.

Thanks in advance—your comments will help us to continue publishing the best books available on computer topics in today's market.

Lorna Gentry
Product Development Specialist
Que Corporation
201 West 103rd St.
Indianapolis, Indiana 46290
USA

CONTENTS

INTRODUCTION

Microsoft Outlook is an e-mail program and much more. With Outlook, you can communicate throughout your office with e-mail, but you can also schedule meetings and invite your coworkers, create task lists for yourself and others, store documents in public folders that everyone can access, and communicate over the Internet. Outlook provides accessibility and flexibility for you and your coworkers.

THE WHAT AND WHY OF OUTLOOK

Outlook can help you organize your work on a day-to-day basis. Using Outlook, you can do the following:

- Create task lists
- Manage your calendar
- Log phone calls and other important events in your journal
- Make notes to remind yourself of important tasks

Additionally, Outlook can help you communicate with others and share your workload. When you and your coworkers use the combined features of Outlook and Microsoft Office, you can:

- Schedule meetings and invite coworkers
- Communicate with others using e-mail
- Import and export files
- Share data and documents through public folders
- Communicate with others over the Internet

Outlook is easy to learn and offers many advantages and benefits in return. This book can help you understand the possibilities awaiting you with Outlook.

This book concentrates on using Outlook in a Windows 95 workstation on which Microsoft Office is also installed. Note, however, that you can also install Outlook on a computer running Windows NT 4.0.

WHY THE *10 MINUTE GUIDE TO OUTLOOK 97*?

The *10 Minute Guide to Outlook 97* can save you precious time while you get to know the program. Each lesson is designed to be completed in 10 minutes or less, so you'll be up to snuff in basic Outlook skills quickly.

Although you can jump around among lessons, starting at the beginning is a good plan. The bare-bones basics are covered first, and more advanced topics are covered later. If you need help installing Outlook, see the next section for instructions.

INSTALLING OUTLOOK

You can install Outlook to a workstation running Windows 95 or Windows NT 4.0. (Outlook will *not* run on a computer running Windows for Workgroups, Windows 3.x, or Windows NT 3.5.) In addition, you can install Outlook in conjunction with Microsoft Office 97, or you can install just the Outlook program.

To install Outlook, follow these steps:

1. Start your computer. Then insert the Microsoft Office CD in the CD-ROM drive.

2. Choose Start, Run. Or, open the CD and click the Setup icon.

3. In the Run dialog box, type the letter of the CD-ROM drive, followed by **setup** (for example, **e:\setup**). If necessary, use the Browse button to locate and select the CD-ROM drive and the setup.exe program.

4. When Setup prompts you, enter your name and organization. Then confirm that they are correct.

5. Choose either the Typical or the Custom option.

6. Follow the on-screen instructions to complete the installation.

CONVENTIONS USED IN THIS BOOK

To help you move through the lessons easily, these conventions are used:

On-screen text	On-screen text appears in bold type.
Text you should type	Information you need to type appears in bold colored type.
Items you select	Commands, options, and icons you are to select and keys you are to press appear in colored type.

In telling you to choose menu commands, this book uses the format *menu title, menu command*. For example, the statement "choose File, Properties" means to "open the File menu and select the Properties command."

In addition to those conventions the *10 Minute Guide to Outlook 97* uses the following icons to identify helpful information:

 Plain English   New or unfamiliar terms are defined in (you got it) "plain English."

Timesaver Tips   Read these tips for ideas that can help you cut corners and confusion.

Panic Button   This icon identifies areas where new users often run into trouble; these tips offer practical solutions to those problems.

Acknowledgments

A lot of hard work went into completing this project, and I'd like to thank all of those involved. First and foremost, my gratitude goes to my acquisitions editor, Martha O'Sullivan. Martha's efficiency, planning, and friendliness make writing for her a pleasure. Thanks, too, to the product development specialist, Faithe Wempen, who is especially perceptive and astute (perhaps because she is also an author). Thanks to Lorna Gentry and to the production editor, Audra Gable, for their guidance and attention to detail. Finally, thanks to Herb Feltner for ensuring the technical consistency and accuracy of this book.

Trademarks

All terms mentioned in this book that are known to be trademarks have been appropriately capitalized. Que cannot attest to the accuracy of this information. Use of a term in this book should not be regarded as affecting the validity of any trademark or service mark.

NAVIGATING OUTLOOK

1

In this lesson, you learn to start and exit Outlook, identify parts of the Outlook screen, and use the mouse to get around the program.

STARTING OUTLOOK

You start Outlook from the Windows desktop. After starting the program, you can leave it open on your screen, or you can minimize it. Either way, you can access it at any time during your work day.

To start Microsoft Outlook, follow these steps:

1. From the Windows desktop, click the Start button and choose Programs, Microsoft Outlook. (If you have customized your Start menu, Outlook may appear within a folder, such as a Microsoft Office folder on the Programs menu.) Or if you have one, you can double-click the shortcut icon on the desktop.

2. If the Choose Profile dialog box appears, click OK to accept the default profile and open Microsoft Outlook. Figure 1.1 shows the Outlook screen that appears. (In Windows NT, Outlook cannot detect an existing e-mail provider. The user is prompted to set up the profile. If you need help, see your system administrator.)

 Profile Information about you and your communications services that is created automatically when you install Outlook. The profile includes your name, user ID, post office, and so on.

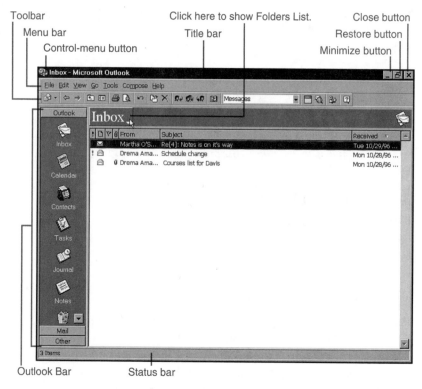

Toolbar
Menu bar
Control-menu button
Click here to show Folders List.
Title bar
Close button
Restore button
Minimize button

Outlook Bar   Status bar

FIGURE 1.1   The Outlook screen includes many icons and items you'll use in your daily routine.

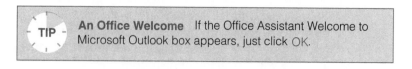

An Office Welcome If the Office Assistant Welcome to Microsoft Outlook box appears, just click OK.

UNDERSTANDING THE SCREEN

The Outlook screen includes items you can use to navigate and operate the program. If you do not see some of the items listed below on your screen, open the View menu and select the command for the appropriate element (such as Toolbars, Status Bar, Folders List, or Outlook Bar). A check mark in front of an item means the item is currently showing. Table 1.1 describes the elements you see in the opening screen.

TABLE 1.1   ELEMENTS OF THE OUTLOOK WINDOW

ELEMENT	DESCRIPTION
Title bar	Includes the name of the application and current folder, plus the Windows Minimize, Maximize, and Close buttons.
Control-menu button	Provides such commands as Move, Size, Minimize, and Close, with which you control the Outlook window.
Minimize button	Reduces the Outlook window to a button on the taskbar; to restore the window to its original size, click the button on the taskbar.
Maximize button	Enlarges the Outlook window to cover the Windows desktop. When the window is maximized, the Maximize button changes to a Restore button that you can click to return the window to its previous size.
Close (X) button	Closes the Outlook program.
Menu bar	Contains menus of commands you can use to perform tasks in the program.
Toolbar	Includes icons that serve as shortcuts for common commands, such as creating a new message or printing a message. (See the inside back cover for a description of each tool.)
Folders List	Displays the current folder. Click this to display a list of Personal Folders you can open.

continues

Table 1.1   Continued

Element	Description
Outlook Bar	Displays icons representing folders: Inbox, Calendar, Contacts, and so on. Click an icon to change to the folder it names.
Status bar	Displays information about what's in the main part of the window.

Finding a Toolbar Button's Purpose   You can hold
TIP   the mouse pointer over any toolbar button to view a description of the tool's function.

Using the Mouse in Outlook

As with most Windows-based programs, you can use the mouse in Outlook to select items, open mail and folders, move items, and so on. In general, clicking selects an item, and double-clicking selects it *and* performs some action on it (like displaying its contents).

In addition to clicking and double-clicking, there are some special mouse actions you can use in Outlook. First, to move an object to another position on the screen (to transfer a mail message to another folder, for example), you can *drag* the object with the mouse. To drag an object to a new location on-screen, point to the object and press and hold down the left mouse button. Move the mouse pointer to the new location, and then release the mouse button.

As another example, you can display a shortcut menu by clicking the right mouse button when pointing to an item. For instance, you can right-click a folder in the Outlook Bar or a piece of mail. A shortcut menu appears, offering common commands relating to that particular item.

Finally, you can act upon multiple items at once by selecting them before issuing a command. To select multiple contiguous items, hold down the Shift key and click the first and last items you want to select. To select noncontiguous items (those that are not adjacent to each other), hold down the Ctrl key and click each item.

If You Must Use the Keyboard   You can use the keyboard to move around Outlook and to access many, but not all, of its features. For example, to open a menu with the keyboard, press the Alt key and then press the underlined letter in the menu name (press Alt+F to open the File menu, for instance). This book concentrates on using the mouse to perform tasks in Outlook; however, I'll include some keyboard shortcuts in tips along the way.

EXITING OUTLOOK

When you're finished with Outlook, you can close the program in a couple of different ways. To close Outlook, do one of the following:

- Choose File, Exit (to remain connected to the mail program).

- Choose File, Exit and Log Off (to disconnect from the mail program).

- Double-click the application's Control-menu button.

- Click the application's Control-menu button and choose Close from the menu.

- Press Alt+F4.

- Click the Close (X) button at the right end of Outlook's title bar.

 Do I Need to Log Off or Not? You will eventually need to log off; however, you may want to remain attached to the mail server to receive mail during your work day.

In this lesson, you learned about the Outlook screen, how to start and exit Outlook, and how to use the mouse to get around the program. In the next lesson, you will learn to open menus, select commands, and use dialog boxes and the toolbar.

GETTING STARTED WITH OUTLOOK

2

In this lesson, you learn to open menus and select commands, use dialog boxes, and use toolbars in Outlook.

USING MENUS AND SELECTING COMMANDS

As do most Windows applications, Outlook supplies pull-down menus that contain the commands you use to work in Outlook. Each menu contains a list of commands that relate to the operation of the program. For example, the Edit menu contains such commands as Cut, Copy, Paste, and Clear. Some menus change depending on the task you're performing. For example, the Compose menu you see when you're working in the Inbox folder changes to the Calendar menu when you switch to the Calendar folder. Those changing menus contain commands that enable you to work in a specific folder.

 Folder A folder is a container of sorts that holds items related to the folder's name. For example, the Inbox folder holds your e-mail messages, and the Calendar folder holds your appointments and meetings. Folders are displayed in the Outlook Bar.

To open a menu, either click it or press and hold the Alt key and press the key for the underlined letter in the menu name. Figure 2.1 shows an open menu.

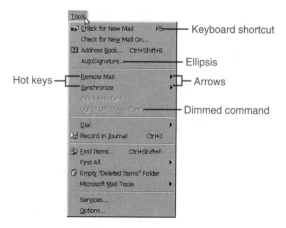

Figure 2.1   Pull-down menus contain commands you use to work in Outlook.

Click a command to select it from an open menu, or press the key for the underlined letter in the command's name (the *hot key*). If an arrow appears to the right of the command, choosing that command leads to a secondary menu; click the command you want in the secondary menu or press its hot key to activate it.

 Hot Key   The underlined letter in a menu name, command name, or other option that you press (often in combination with the Alt key) to activate that option. Also referred to as the *accelerator key*.

Menus can contain a number of elements along with the commands. For example, some commands have hot keys you can use to select them from the keyboard, and some have keyboard shortcuts with which you can bypass the menu altogether. In addition, certain symbols may appear in a menu to give you an indication as to what will happen when you activate the command. Table 2.1 describes the command indicators you might see in a menu.

TABLE 2.1   COMMAND INDICATORS

ELEMENT	DESCRIPTION
Arrow	Indicates that another menu, called a secondary or cascading menu, will appear when you select the command.
Ellipsis	Indicates that a dialog box will appear when you select that command.
Hot key	Marks the letter whose key you press to activate the menu or the command using the keyboard.
Check mark	Indicates that an option or command is selected or active.
Shortcut	Provides a keyboard shortcut you can use to activate the command without accessing the menu; you cannot use the shortcut if the menu is open but you can remember it for use at another time (when the menu is not open).
Dimmed command	Indicates that the command cannot be accessed at the current time. (For example, you cannot tell Outlook to copy unless you've selected something for it to copy; so if nothing is selected, the Copy command is not available.)

Cancel a Menu   To close a smenu without choosing a command from it, point to any blank area of the Outlook window and click once, or press the Esc key twice.

USING DIALOG BOXES

Often, selecting a menu command causes Outlook to display a dialog box. You can use dialog boxes to set more options and make specific choices related to the menu command. Each type of box contains certain elements you need to understand in order to use it.

Figure 2.2 shows the Options dialog box, in which you can customize Outlook for your personal needs. This dialog box contains most of the elements common to Outlook dialog boxes. Table 2.2 describes those elements and tells you how to use them.

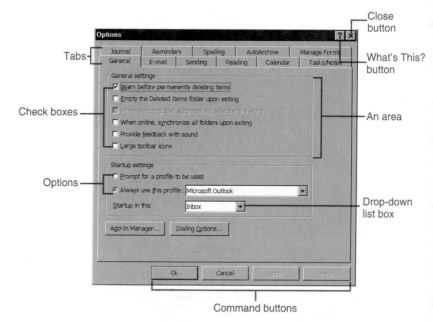

FIGURE 2.2 Use dialog boxes to make additional choices related to the selected menu command.

 Tabs   The tabs in a dialog box are similar to the tabs in a drawer full of file folders. Select a tab to see information related to the tab's title.

TABLE 2.2   DIALOG BOX ELEMENTS

ELEMENT	DESCRIPTION
Tab	A "page" of the dialog box, which contains a group of related options. Click a tab to switch to it.
Area	A grouping of elements on a tab or in a dialog box that is surrounded by a box.
Check box	Toggles an individual option on or off.
Option buttons	These enable you to choose one option from several options in a group. When you select one option, the previously selected option becomes deselected.
Drop-down list box	Displays one option from a list; click the arrow to the right of the box, and the box drops down to display the list.
Command button	Closes the dialog box or leads to another related dialog box containing more options.
What's This button	Presents a brief explanation or definition of the elements in any dialog box. Click the ? in the title bar of the dialog box, and the mouse pointer changes to a question mark. Click the pointer on an item in the dialog box to get more information about it. (In NT, not all dialog boxes contain the What's This? button.)
Close button	Closes the dialog box and cancels any changes you made to its contents.
List box	Displays a list of options so you can see more than one choice at a time.
Text box	Enables you to enter a selection by typing it in the box.
Check list	Enables you to select one or more items from a displayed list of options.

To use a dialog box, you make your selections as described in Table 2.2, and then choose a command button. The following list describes the functions of the most common command buttons:

- OK or Done accepts and puts into effect the selections in the dialog box, and then closes the dialog box.

- Cancel cancels the changes you've made in the dialog box and closes it, as does the Close (X) button at the right end of the title bar.

- Apply employs the changes you made to the options in a tab but leaves the dialog box open for you to choose other tabs and options. If you cancel a dialog box after choosing Apply, the changes made before choosing Apply remain intact.

- Browse (or any other button with an ellipsis following the button's name) displays another dialog box.

- Open (or any other button with a command on it) performs that command.

- Help displays information about the dialog box and its options.

I Can't Get Rid of the Dialog Box   Once you've opened a dialog box, you must cancel or accept any change you make and close that dialog box before you can continue your work in Outlook.

USING TOOLBAR SHORTCUTS

As do other Windows programs, Microsoft Outlook includes toolbars you can use to perform common tasks quickly. Outlook supplies some specific toolbar buttons that appear depending on your location in the program and the task you're going to perform. When you're in the Inbox, for example, the Reply and Forward toolbar buttons appear. On the other hand, some toolbar buttons—including the Folders List and Print buttons—are always displayed.

To display or hide the toolbar, choose View, Toolbars, Standard. (The Standard option is a *toggle*, which means it works like a light switch. If the option is turned on (checked) and you click it, the check mark disappears and the option is turned off—and vice versa.) In addition to the Standard toolbar, Outlook offers a toolbar called Remote that has the Connect, Disconnect, and Mark to Retrieve buttons, and other tools you can use when you're calling the office via a modem with Outlook.

To find out which command a toolbar button represents, hold the mouse pointer over the icon, and a description appears containing the name of the menu command for which the icon is a shortcut. Figure 2.3 shows a description for the Move to Folder button, which is the shortcut for a command on the Edit menu.

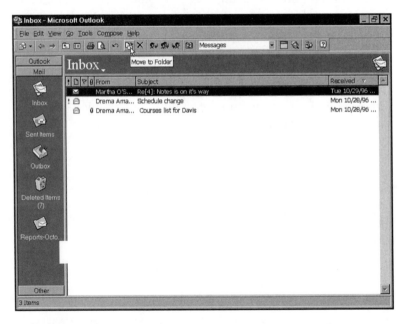

FIGURE 2.3 Toolbar button descriptions tell you what the icons do.

To activate a tool on a toolbar, simply click it.

In this lesson, you learned to open menus and select commands, use dialog boxes, and use toolbars in Outlook. In the next lesson, you learn to use the Outlook tools.

USING OUTLOOK'S TOOLS

In this lesson, you learn to change views in Outlook, use the Outlook Bar, and use the Folders List.

USING THE OUTLOOK BAR

Outlook's components are organized by folder. There is a folder for e-mail, a folder for the calendar, and so on. The Outlook Bar is a tool you can use to quickly change folders in Outlook. The icons in the Outlook Bar represent all of the folders available to you and provide shortcuts to getting to the contents of those folders. Figure 3.1 shows the Outlook Bar.

There are three groups within the Outlook Bar: Outlook, Mail, and Other. Each group contains related folders in which you can work. The Outlook group contains folders for working with different features in Outlook, such as the Inbox, Calendar, Tasks, and so on. The Mail group contains folders for organizing and managing your mail. And the Other group contains folders on your computer for working outside of Outlook. To switch from one group to another, click the Outlook, Mail, or Other button in the Outlook Bar. The Outlook group is displayed by default.

THE OUTLOOK GROUP FOLDERS

The Outlook group's folders in the Outlook Bar enable you to access your work in Outlook. That includes your mail messages, appointments, address list, and so on. Table 3.1 describes each of the folders within the Outlook group.

Group buttons   Selected folder   Contents of selected folder

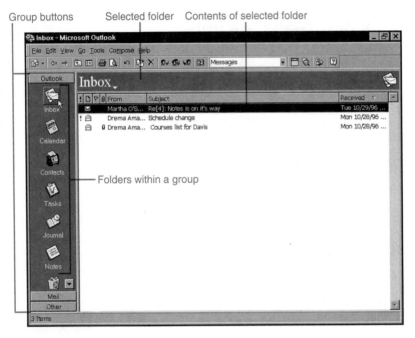

FIGURE 3.1   Use the Outlook Bar to view various items in your work.

TABLE 3.1   OUTLOOK GROUP FOLDERS

FOLDER	DESCRIPTION
Inbox	Includes messages you've sent and received via e-mail.
Calendar	Contains your appointments, events, scheduled meetings, and so on.
Contacts	Lists names and addresses of the people with whom you communicate.
Tasks	Includes any tasks on your to-do list.
Journal	Contains all journal entries, such as phone logs, meeting notes, and so on.
Notes	Lists notes you write yourself or others.
Deleted Items	Includes any items you've deleted from other folders.

THE MAIL GROUP FOLDERS

The Mail group folders provide a method of organizing your incoming and outgoing e-mail messages. Table 3.2 describes each folder in the Mail group.

TABLE 3.2   MAIL GROUP FOLDERS

FOLDER	DESCRIPTION
Inbox	Contains all received messages.
Sent Items	Stores all messages you've sent.
Outbox	Contains messages to be sent.
Deleted Items	Holds any deleted mail messages.

THE OTHER GROUP FOLDERS

The Other group contains folders that are on your computer but not within Outlook: My Computer, My Documents, and Favorites. This enables you to access a document or information in any of those areas so that you can attach it to a message, add notes to it, or otherwise use it in Outlook.

For example, with My Computer, you can view the contents of both hard and floppy disks, CD-ROM drives and so on (see Figure 3.2). Double-click a drive in the window to view its folders and files. Double-click a folder to view its contents as well. Then you can attach files to messages or otherwise use the files on your hard drive with the Outlook features.

USING THE FOLDERS LIST

Outlook provides another method of viewing the folders within Outlook and your system: the Folders List. The Folders List displays the folders within any of the three groups (Outlook, Mail, or Other). From the list, you can select the folder you want. To use the Folders List, first select the group you want to view from the Outlook Bar. Then click the Folder List button to display the list (see Figure 3.3).

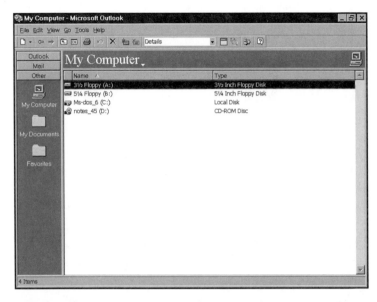

FIGURE 3.2 View your entire system through the My Computer folder in Outlook.

Click here to display the Folders List.

FIGURE 3.3 The Folders List shows all folders in the group you selected.

Choose any folder from the list, and the folder's contents appear. If you display another folder in the Information screen, double-click it to display its contents.

CHANGING VIEWS

In Outlook, views give you different ways to look at the same information in a folder. Each view presents the information in a different format and organization so you can get the most from the program. The following list outlines the view types and provides a brief description of each. A view type determines the basic structure of the view; within each view type, you can change the way you see the information.

Table view type. Presents items in a grid of sorts—in rows and columns. Use this view type to view mail messages, tasks, and details about any item.

Timeline view type. Displays items as icons arranged in chronological order from left to right on a time scale. Use this to view journal entries and other items in this type of view.

Day/week/month view type. Displays items in a calendar view in blocks of time. Use this type for meetings and scheduled tasks.

Card view type. Presents items like cards in a card file. Use this to view contacts.

Icon view type. Provides graphic icons to represent tasks, notes, calendars, and so on.

 TIP **Looking at the Inbox** The default view for your Inbox looks like Table view type, in which items appear in columns and rows, but it is called Messages with AutoPreview.

Each folder—Inbox, Calendar, Contacts, and so on—displays its contents in a particular view type, as previously described.

Additionally, within each view type, you have a choice of views that further fine-tune the presentation of the information on-screen. You can change a view by clicking the Current View drop-down list on the standard toolbar (see Figure 3.4).

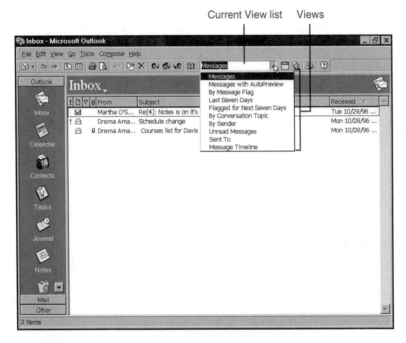

FIGURE 3.4 Select a view to change the format of the information.

As you can see in Figure 3.4, within the Table view type of the Inbox, you can change views so that you can see all messages, messages from the last seven days, messages organized by sender, unread messages only, and so on. Similarly, the Calendar folder—which is arranged in the Day/Week/Month view type by default—enables you to view active appointments, events, recurring appointments, and so on (see Figure 3.5).

As you work your way through this book, you'll see examples of each view type. When you change folders in Outlook, take a look at the available views in the Current View drop-down list.

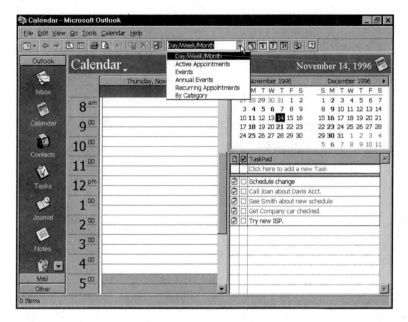

FIGURE 3.5   You can choose how to view the contents of the Calendar folder.

In this lesson, you learned to change views in Outlook, use the Outlook Bar, and use the Folders List. In the next lesson, you learn to get help in Outlook.

Getting Help

In this lesson, you learn to use the Office Assistant, to search for help on specific topics, and to use other Help features.

Using the Office Assistant

You've probably noticed the Office Assistant: he's the paper clip in a window all his own. You can use the Office Assistant to help you with procedures, explanations, and tasks you perform in Outlook.

To use the Office Assistant, do one of the following:

- Click the Assistant's window.

- Choose Help, Microsoft Outlook Help.

- Press F1.

The Assistant displays the help box shown in Figure 4.1. Office Assistant's help is context-sensitive; thus, depending on where you are in the program, the Assistant tries to offer help on related topics. If you need help on one of the suggested topics, click one of the blue option buttons.

Context-Sensitive A help feature that senses where you are in the program—in the Inbox, using the Calendar, or creating a message, for example—and offers help on topics that are related to your current task.

If you need help on another topic, you can enter the topic in the text box and click Search. You might, for example, enter the word "Print" (or "File" or any other topic for which you need help). When the Office Assistant box appears, it contains options about the related topics.

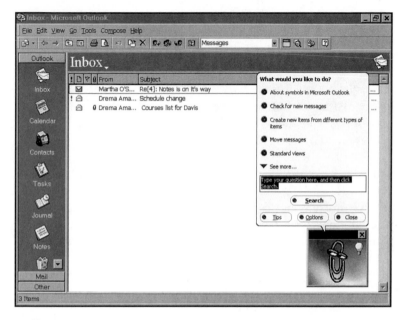

FIGURE 4.1 Use the Office Assistant to get context-sensitive help in Outlook.

To close the Office Assistant, click the Close button or click outside of the help box.

Tricks of the Trade Click the light bulb in the Assistant's window to see a tip; click the Next button to view another tip; click the Close button to close the tip box.

You can right-click the Office Assistant and choose Hide the Assistant from the shortcut menu; you can also change the animated icon that represents the Assistant by right-clicking and choosing Choose Assistant from the shortcut menu. In the Office Assistant dialog box, you can choose the Assistant character you like. You also can choose options for the Assistant, including the type of tips displayed, the type of help you get with the Assistant, and so on.

USING THE CONTENTS FEATURE

Use the Contents help to view Outlook's Help Topics. The Help Topics function as a sort of on-screen user manual, providing a series of "books" with "chapters" you can read. You can find out how to print, use the calendar, format text, share information, and more.

To use the Contents feature, follow these steps:

1. Choose Help, Contents and Index. The Help Topics window appears (see Figure 4.2).

FIGURE 4.2 Find general information about tasks and procedures in the Contents section of Help.

2. Double-click a topic in the list, or click the topic and click the Open button. A more detailed list of topics appears, from which you can choose the document you want to view.

3. Double-click any topic, and another Help window appears with the procedure or explanation of the topic you selected. Figure 4.3 shows the Help window that results from choosing "Printing," "Print," and then "Print an Item."

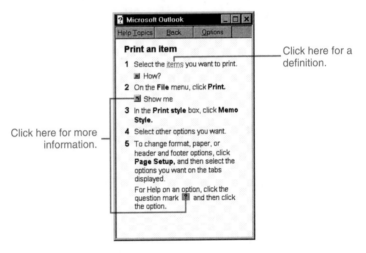

Figure **4.3** Let Help guide you through various processes in Outlook.

4. (Optional) To view the definition of any underlined word in a Help window, click the underlined word. Click the word a second time to close the definition box.

Help While You Work By default, the Help window stays on top of your work so you can refer to it as you follow the steps. If you'd prefer that the Help window not stay on top, open the Options menu, choose Keep Help on Top, and then select Not on Top.

5. (Optional) To find out more information, choose any of the gray buttons displayed in the Help text (see Figure 4.3).

6. When you're finished with Help, you can do any of the following:

Print the topic by choosing Options, Print Topic.

Click the Back button to view the previous Help window.

Click the Help Topics button to go back to the Help Topics window.

Click the Close (X) button to close Help.

SEARCHING WITH THE INDEX

Using the Help index, you can view or search through an alphabetical list for tasks and topics. *Topics* include Outlook features (usually in the form of nouns) such as Bulleted lists, Modem, or OLE. *Tasks* are actions you can perform in Outlook (in the form of verbs) such as Copying, Inserting, or Linking.

After you find the general task or topic you want in the Help Index, you can select a more specific topic or any of the related topics listed below it (see Figure 4.4).

FIGURE 4.4   When you look up a task such as Copying, you can choose from several related topics (files, tasks, messages, etc.).

To search for specific help using the Index, follow these steps:

1. In Outlook, choose Help, Contents and Index. The Help Topics window appears.

2. Click the Index tab.

3. In the text box, enter as many letters of the topic as necessary to narrow the search; as you type, the topic list jumps to the available listings that match what you type.

4. To view a specific topic, double-click it. Sometimes a dialog box appears listing more related topics; double-click the topic you want to view.

5. The Help window that appears is similar to the Help window that appears when you use the Contents help. You can print or close the Help window, or you can return to the Index Help window when you're done.

USING THE FIND TAB IN HELP

The Find tab lets you look for help in a different way. Find provides a method for narrowing a search of topics. For example, you might want information about printing. If you type the word "print" in the text box, a list of related words (such as printer, printing, prints, and so on) appears. You can let Outlook search for all of those topics, or you can narrow the search by typing more specific text such as "printed" or "prints."

To use the Find tab, follow these steps:

1. Choose Help, Contents and Index. The Help window appears.

2. Click the Find tab.

TIP **Setting Up Find** The first time you use the Find tab, Outlook displays a dialog box asking if you want to set up the Find Help. Click the Next button, and a second dialog box appears. Click the Finish button, and Outlook sets up the Help database for you.

3. In the 1 Type the Word(s) You Want to Find text box, enter a word, topic, or phrase.

4. In the 2 Select Some Matching Words to Narrow Your Search list, click the topic you want to search for (see Figure 4.5). (To select multiple words listed next to each other, hold down the Shift key and click the first and last words. To select multiple items that are not adjacent, hold the Ctrl key and click each one.)

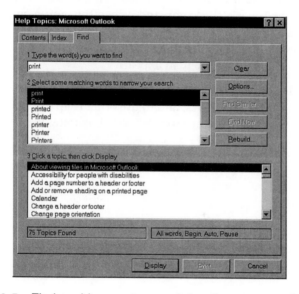

FIGURE 4.5 Find enables you to search for phrases as well as one-word topics.

5. Choose the topic you want from the 3 Click a Topic list box. Then click the Display button, and Outlook displays the Help window containing information related to the selected topic.

6. When you finish, click the Close (X) button to close the Help window or return to the Help Topics.

WHAT'S THIS?

In most of its dialog boxes, Outlook includes a handy tool called a What's This button. This is the question mark button that appears at the right end of the title bar next to the Close (X) button. You can click the What's This button and then click on any item in the dialog box to see an explanation or definition of the selected element. Click again to hide the help box.

Another way to use this feature is to open the Help menu and choose the What's This command. When the mouse pointer changes to a pointer with a question mark, click on anything in the Outlook window about which you have a question, and a Help box explaining the item appears.

In this lesson, you learned to use the Office Assistant, to search for help on specific topics, and to use other Help features. In the next lesson, you will learn to work with incoming mail.

WORKING WITH INCOMING MAIL

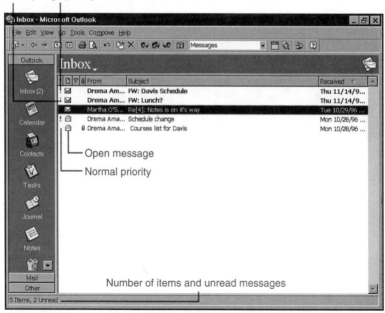

LESSON 5

In this lesson, you learn to read your mail, save an attachment, answer mail, and close a message.

READING MAIL

When you log on to Outlook, your Inbox folder appears, and any new messages you've received are waiting for you (see Figure 5.1).

Low priority High priority

Open message

Normal priority

Number of items and unread messages

FIGURE 5.1 Review the sender and subject before opening mail.

As you can see in this figure, the Inbox provides important information about each message. For example, two messages have been labeled as high priority, one is low priority, and one message has an attachment. You'll learn about priorities and attachments in Lesson 9, "Setting Mail Options." In addition, the Status bar at the bottom of the Inbox window indicates how many items the Inbox folder contains and how many of those items are unread.

Welcome! The first time you log on, you may find a welcome message from Microsoft in your Inbox. After you read the message, you can delete it by selecting it and pressing the Delete key.

To open and read your messages, follow these steps:

1. Double-click a mail message to open it. Figure 5.2 shows an open message.

Read previous mail item. Read next mail item.

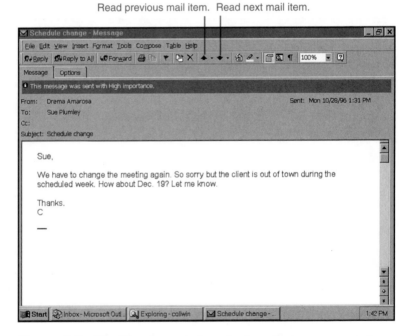

FIGURE 5.2 The Message window displays the message and some tools for handling this message or moving on to another.

2. To read the next or previous mail message in the Inbox, click the Previous Item or the Next Item button on the toolbar. Or you can open the View menu, choose Previous or Next, and choose Item.

Item   Outlook uses the word "item" to describe a mail message, an attached file, an appointment or meeting, a task, and so on. "Item" is a generic term in Outlook that describes the currently selected element.

You can mark messages as read or unread by choosing Edit, Mark as Read or Mark as Unread. Outlook automatically marks messages as read when you open them. But you might want to mark messages yourself once in a while (as a reminder, for example). Additionally, you can mark all of the messages in the Inbox as read at one time by choosing Edit, Mark All as Read. You might want to mark mail messages as read so you don't read them again; you might want to mark important mail as unread so you'll be sure to open it and read it again.

No Mail?   If you don't see any new mail in your Inbox, choose Tools, Check for New Mail, and Outlook will update your mail for you. Choose Tools, Check for New Mail On to specify a service other than the default. See Lesson 24 for more information.

SAVING AN ATTACHMENT

You will often receive messages that have files or other items attached. In the Inbox list of messages, an attachment is represented by a paper clip icon beside the message. You'll want to save any attachments sent to you so you can open, modify, print, or otherwise use the document. Messages can contain multiple attachments. To save an attachment, follow these steps:

1. Open the message containing an attachment by double-clicking the message. The attachment appears as an icon in the message text (see Figure 5.3)

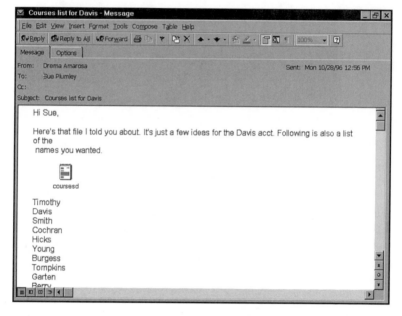

FIGURE 5.3   An icon represents the attached file.

2. (Optional) You can open the attachment from within the message by double-clicking the icon. The application in which the document was created opens and displays the document in the window. Close the application by choosing File, Exit.

3. In the message, select the attachment you want to save and choose File, Save Attachments. The Save Attachments dialog box appears (see Figure 5.4).

4. Choose the folder in which you want to save the attachment and click Save. (You can change the name of the file if you want.) The dialog box closes, and you're returned to the message window. You can open the attachment at any time from the application in which it was created.

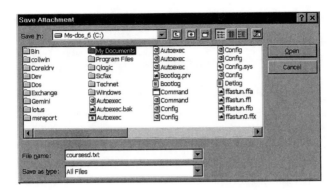

FIGURE 5.4 Save the attachment to a convenient folder.

ANSWERING MAIL

You might want to reply to a message after you read it. The Message window enables you to answer a message immediately, or at a later time if you prefer. To reply to any given message, open the message and follow these steps:

 1. Click the Reply button or choose Compose, Reply. The Reply Message window appears, with the original message in the message text area and the sender of the message already filled in for you (see Figure 5.5).

 TIP **Reply to All** If you receive a message that has also been sent to others—as either a message or a "carbon copy" (Cc)—you can click the Reply to All button to send your reply to each person who received the message.

2. The insertion point is in the message text area, ready for you to enter your reply. Enter the text.

 3. When you finish your reply, click the Send button or choose File, Send. Outlook sends the message.

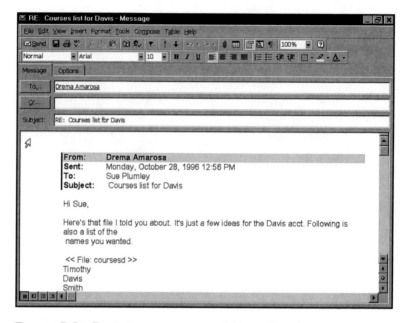

FIGURE 5.5 Reply to a message quickly and easily.

You also can send a reply from the Inbox, without opening the message. Suppose, for example, you already read the message and closed it, but now you've decided you want to reply. Select the message in the Inbox list and click the Reply button. The Reply Message window appears with the original message in the text area and the sender's name in the To area. Enter your text and send the message as you learned in the previous steps.

TIP

Reminder The next time you open a message to which you've replied, you'll see a reminder at the top of the Message tab that tells you the date and time you sent your reply.

PRINTING MAIL

You can print mail messages whether they're open or not. To print an unopened message, select the message in the message list of the Inbox or other folder and choose File, Print. If the message is already open, you can follow the steps below:

1. Open the message in Outlook.

2. Use one of the following methods to tell Outlook to print:

   - Click the Print button on the toolbar to print using defaults.

   - Choose the File, Print command to view the Print dialog box.

   - Press Ctrl+P.

3. In the Print dialog box, click OK to print one copy of the entire message using the printer's default settings.

 More Print Info   See Lesson 18, "Printing in Outlook," for detailed information about configuring pages, setting up the printer, and so on.

CLOSING A MESSAGE

When you finish with a message, you can close it in any of the following ways:

- Choose File, Close.

- Click the Control-menu button and click Close.

- Press Alt+F4.

- Click the Close (X) button in the Message window.

In this lesson, you learned to read your mail, save an attachment, answer mail, and close a message. In the next lesson, you will learn to manage your mail messages.

6

LESSON

MANAGING MAIL

In this lesson, you learn to delete and undelete messages, forward messages, and organize messages by saving them to folders.

DELETING MAIL

You may want to store some important messages, but you'll definitely want to delete much of the mail you receive. Once you've answered a question or responded to a request, you probably won't have need for a reminder of that transaction. You can easily delete messages in Outlook when you're finished with them.

To delete a mail message that is open, do one of the following:

- Choose Edit, Delete.

- Press Ctrl+D.

 • Click the Delete button on the toolbar.

If you have modified the message in any way, a confirmation message appears from the Office Assistant or as a message dialog box. Otherwise, the message is deleted without warning.

If you're in the Inbox and you want to delete one or more messages from the message list, select the single message to delete (or hold down Ctrl and click each message). Then do one of the following:

- Press the Delete key.

 • Click the Delete button on the toolbar.

UNDELETING ITEMS

If you change your mind and want to get back items you've deleted, you can usually retrieve them from the Deleted Items folder. By default, when you delete an item, it doesn't disappear from your system; it merely moves to the Deleted Items folder. Items stay in the Deleted Items folder until you delete them from that folder—at which point they are unrecoverable.

To retrieve a deleted item from the Deleted Items folder, follow these steps:

1. Click the Deleted Items icon in the Outlook Bar to open the folder.

2. Select the items you want to retrieve and drag them to the folder containing the same type of items on the Outlook Bar. Alternatively, you can choose Edit, Move to Folder and choose the folder to which you want to move the selected items and click OK.

EMPTYING THE DELETED ITEMS FOLDER

If you're really sure you want to delete the items in the Deleted Items folder, you can erase them from your system. To delete items in the Deleted Items folder, follow these steps:

1. In the Outlook Bar, choose the Outlook group and then select the Deleted Items folder. All deleted items in that folder appear in the message list, as shown in Figure 6.1.

2. To permanently delete an item, select it in the Deleted Items folder and click the Delete tool button or choose Edit, Delete. (You can choose more than one item at a time by holding the **Shift** or **Ctrl** key as you click the items.)

3. Outlook displays a confirmation dialog box asking if you're sure you want to permanently delete the message. Choose Yes to delete the selected item.

4. To switch back to the Inbox or another folder, select the folder from either the Outlook Bar or the Folders List.

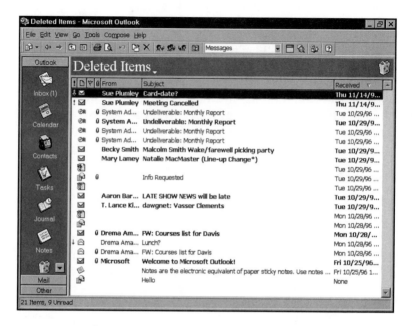

FIGURE 6.1   Deleted messages remain in the Deleted Items folder until you permanently delete them.

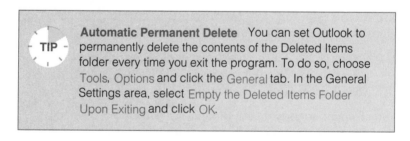

Automatic Permanent Delete   You can set Outlook to permanently delete the contents of the Deleted Items folder every time you exit the program. To do so, choose Tools, Options and click the General tab. In the General Settings area, select Empty the Deleted Items Folder Upon Exiting and click OK.

Forwarding Mail

Suppose you want to forward mail you receive from a coworker to another person who has an interest in the message. You can forward any message you receive, and you can even add comments to the message if you want.

Forward Mail When you forward mail, you send a message you received to another person on the network; you
can add your own comments to the forwarded mail if you
want.

You forward an open message or a message selected in the message list in the Inbox in the same way. To forward mail, follow
these steps:

 1. Select or open the message you want to forward. Then
click the Forward button or choose Compose, Forward.
The FW Message dialog box appears (see Figure 6.2).

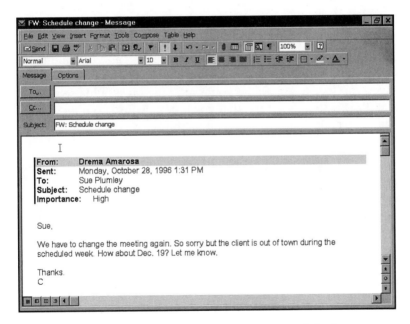

FIGURE 6.2 When you forward a message, the original message
appears at the bottom of the message window.

2. In the To text box, enter the names of the people to
whom you want to forward the mail. (If you want to
choose a person's name from a list, click the To... button
to display the Select Names dialog box, and then select

the person's name.) Lesson 7 explains more about using the Address Book. If you enter multiple names in the To box, separate the names with a semi-colon and a space.

3. (Optional) In the Cc text box, enter the names of anyone to whom you want to forward *copies* of the message (or click the Cc... button and choose the name from the list that appears).

4. In the message area of the window, enter any message you want to send with the forwarded text. The text you type will be a different color.

 5. Click the Send button or choose File, Send.

SAVING MAIL TO A FOLDER

Although you'll delete some mail after you read and respond to it, you'll want to save other messages for future reference. You can save a message to any folder you want, but you should use a logical filing system to ensure that you'll be able find each message again later. Outlook offers several methods for organizing your mail.

The easiest method of saving mail to a folder is to move it to one of Outlook's built-in Mail folders (as described in Lesson 3). You can use any of the folders to store your mail, or you can create new folders. Lesson 11, "Organizing Messages," describes how to create your own folders within Outlook.

To move messages to an existing folder, follow these steps:

 1. Select one message (by clicking it) or select multiple messages (by Ctrl+clicking).

 Making Backup Copies   You can also copy a message to another folder as a backup. To do so, choose Edit, Copy to Folder.

2. Choose Edit, Move to Folder or click the Move to Folder tool button on the toolbar. The Move Items dialog box appears (see Figure 6.3).

3. Select the folder you want to move the item to and click OK. Outlook moves the item to the folder for you.

To view the message(s) you've moved, choose the folder from the Outlook Bar or the Folders List. Then click the item you want to view.

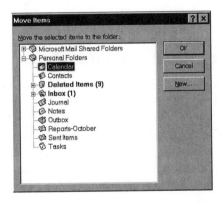

FIGURE 6.3 Choose the folder to which you want to move the selected message(s).

In this lesson, you learned to forward messages, delete messages, and organize messages by saving them to folders. In the next lesson, you will learn to work with address books.

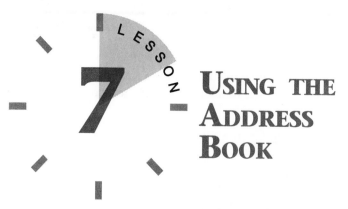

7

USING THE ADDRESS BOOK

In this lesson, you learn to use Outlook's address book with your e-mail.

USING THE POSTOFFICE ADDRESS LIST

All of the names within your organization usually appear on the Postoffice Address List created by your system's mail administrator. Anytime you want to send or forward an e-mail, you can select the recipients from that list instead of typing in their names manually. If you're using Windows NT on a network, you may or may not have access to the Postoffice Address List, depending on your permissions and rights. If you have questions, see your system administrator.

Post Office A directory, usually located on the network server, that contains a mailbox for each e-mail user. When someone sends a message, that message is filed in the recipient's mailbox until the recipient receives the mail and copies, moves, or deletes it.

Postoffice Address List A list of everyone who has a mailbox in the post office; it's controlled by the mail administrator.

Mail Administrator The person who manages the e-mail post office. (This person might also be the network administrator, but it doesn't necessarily have to be the same person.)

To use the Postoffice Address List, choose Tools, Address Book or click the Address Book tool button on the toolbar. The Address Book dialog box appears, as shown in Figure 7.1.

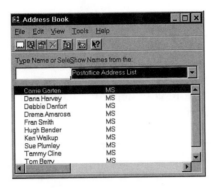

Figure 7.1   View the Postoffice Address List.

The following list outlines some of the ways in which you might use the Address List:

- To view more details about any entry in the Address Book dialog box, double-click the person's name or click the Properties button on the toolbar. The person's Properties dialog box appears, with his or her name, address type, postoffice name, and network type listed on the Address (1) tab. Click OK to close this dialog box and return to the Address Book dialog box.

- Click the Properties toolbar button and choose the Address (2) tab in the person's Properties dialog box to view his or her phone number, office, or department, and any notes or comments that have been added to the description. Click OK to close this dialog box and return to the Address Book dialog box.

- To send a message to someone listed in the Address Book, select the name from the Address List and choose File, New Message. See Lesson 8 for more information.

- If you cannot find a particular name in the list, you can search for it. Choose Tools, Find or click the Find button, and then enter the name for which you're searching in the Find Name Beginning With text box. Click OK to start the search.

USING THE PERSONAL ADDRESS BOOK

The Personal Address Book contains the names and e-mail addresses of people you contact frequently. You may want to include coworkers from your department, or even people from outside of your office (who you contact via Internet addresses).

TIP **Let Outlook Help You Out** You might notice the Outlook Address Book in the list of address books; this book contains entries you create in your Contacts list. For more information about the Contacts list, see Lesson 14.

No Personal Address Book Is Listed? If you do not see a Personal Address Book in the Address Book dialog box, you can easily add it to your resources. Close the address book and choose Tools, Services. In the Services tab of the dialog box, click the Add button, choose the Personal Address Book from the list, and click OK. In the Personal Address Book dialog box, select your preference and click OK. Close the Services dialog box and open the address book again; you'll see the Personal Address Book in the list. You may have to exit and restart Outlook.

To add names to the Personal Address Book, follow these steps:

 1. Choose Tools, Address Book or click the Address Book tool button on the toolbar. The Address Book dialog box appears (refer to Figure 7.1).

 2. To add name(s) from the Postoffice Address List, select the name(s) and click the Add to Personal Address Book button on the toolbar or choose File, Add to Personal Address

Book. The name(s) remain on the Postoffice Address List, but Outlook copies them to your Personal Address Book as well.

3. To view your Personal Address Book, select the Show Names from the drop-down list and choose Personal Address Book. The list changes to display those names you've added to your personal address list, but the dialog box looks the same.

4. To add a completely new address to your Personal Address Book, click the New Entry button or choose File, New Entry. The New Entry dialog box appears (see Figure 7.2).

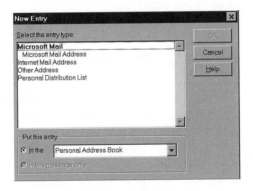

FIGURE 7.2   Choose a source for your new entry.

5. In the Select the Entry Type list, choose from the available options. The options you see will depend on the information systems installed to your network; for example, Microsoft Mail, Internet Mail, or some other service may be available. You can add an address entry that corresponds with one of the available information systems.

Additionally, you can choose to add one of the following two items:

Personal Distribution List   Use this to create one address entry for a group of recipients. When you send mail to the list name, everyone on the list receives the message. You might use this option for grouping department heads, for example.

Other Address   Choose this option to add one new recipient at a time. You can enter a name, e-mail address, and e-mail type for each entry. In addition, you can enter business addresses and phone numbers, and you can add notes and comments to the entry. Use this entry for Internet addresses, for example.

6. When you're done working in your Personal Address Book, close the window by choosing File, Close. You're returned to the Outlook Inbox.

ENTERING AN ADDRESS IN A MESSAGE

You can use either address book to choose the names of recipients to whom you want to send new messages, forward messages, or send a reply. Using the address books also makes sending carbon copies and blind carbon copies easy.

 Blind Carbon Copy   A blind carbon copy (Bcc) of a message is a copy that's sent to someone in secret; the other recipients have no way of knowing that you're sending the message to someone via a blind carbon copy.

To address a message, follow these steps:

1. Choose Compose, New Mail Message from the Outlook Inbox window.

2. In the Message window, click the To button to display the Select Names dialog box.

3. Open the Show Names from the drop-down list box and choose either the Postoffice Address List or the Personal Address Book.

4. From the list that appears on the left, choose the name of the intended recipient and select the To button. Outlook copies the name to the Message Recipients list. (You can add multiple names if you want.)

5. (Optional) Select the names of anyone to whom you want to send a carbon copy and click the Cc button to transfer those names to the Message Recipients list.

6. (Optional) Select the names of anyone to whom you want to send a blind carbon copy and click the Bcc button. Figure 7.3 shows a distribution group listing as the To recipient of a message; in addition, two people are selected to receive blind carbon copies of the same message.

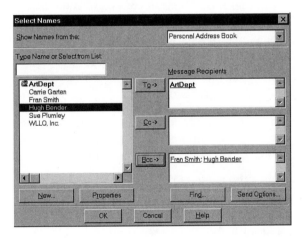

Figure 7.3 Address messages quickly with the Select Names dialog box.

7. Click OK to return to the Message window and complete your message. (For more information about writing messages, see Lesson 8.)

In this lesson, you learned to use the address book with your e-mail. In the next lesson, you will learn to compose a message and format it.

LESSON 8

CREATING MAIL

In this lesson, you learn to compose a message, format text, check your spelling, and send mail.

COMPOSING A MESSAGE

You can send a message to anyone for whom you have an address, whether he or she is in your address book or not. And in addition to sending a message to one or more recipients, you can send copies of a message to others on your address list. (See Lesson 7 for information about addressing a message and sending carbon copies.)

To compose a message, follow these steps:

1. In the Outlook Inbox, click the New Mail Message button or choose Compose, New Mail Message. The Untitled - Message window appears (see Figure 8.1).

2. Enter the name of the recipient in the To text box, or click the To... button and select the name of the recipient from your Address Book. (See Lesson 7 for information about the Address Book.)

3. Enter the name of anyone to whom you want to send a copy of the message in the Cc text box, or click the Cc... button and select a name from the Address Book.

4. In the Subject text box, enter the subject of the message.

5. Click in the text area, and then enter the text of the message. You do not have to press the Enter key at the end of a line; Outlook automatically wraps the text at the end of a line for you. You can use the Delete and Backspace keys to edit the text you enter.

6. When you finish typing the message, you can send the message right away (see "Sending Mail" later in this lesson), or you can check the spelling and formatting as described in the following sections.

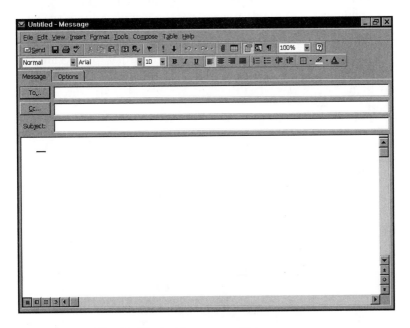

FIGURE 8.1 The Untitled - Message window.

No Address! If you try to compose a message to someone without entering an address, Outlook displays the Check Names dialog box, in which it asks you to create an address. You can search for the name among the existing addresses, or you can create a new address for the name in much the same way you would create a new entry in the Address Book (see Lesson 7).

FORMATTING TEXT

You can change the format of the text in your message to make it more attractive, to make it easier to read, or to add emphasis. Any formatting you do transfers to the recipient with the message if the recipient has Outlook; however, if the recipient doesn't have Outlook, formatting may not transfer.

There are two ways to format text. You can format the text after you type it by selecting it and then choosing a font, size, or other attribute; or you can select the font, size, or other attribute and then enter the text.

To format the text in your message, follow these steps:

1. If the Formatting toolbar is not showing, choose View, Toolbars, Formatting. Figure 8.2 shows a message with the Formatting Toolbar displayed. Table 8.1 shows the buttons on this toolbar.

Formatting toolbar

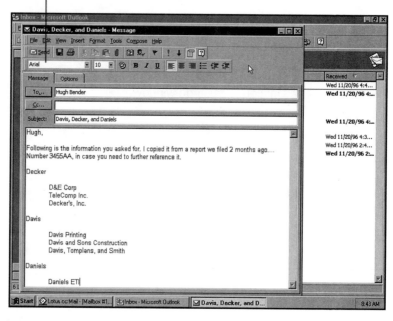

FIGURE 8.2   Use the Formatting toolbar to modify the appearance of your message text.

2. To apply a font to the selected or about-to-be-entered text, click the down arrow in the Font box on the Formatting toolbar. Scroll through the font list, if necessary, to view all fonts on the system, and click the font you want to apply to the text.

Quick Format You can also format text by choosing Format, Font and selecting a font, size, style, and so on from the Font dialog box. You also can assign bullets and alignment to text by choosing Format, Paragraph.

TABLE 8.1 FORMATTING TOOLBAR BUTTONS

BUTTON	NAME
Arial	Font
10	Font Size
(icon)	Font Color
B	Bold
I	Italic
U	Underline
(icon)	Align Left
(icon)	Center
(icon)	Align Right
(icon)	Bullets
(icon)	Decrease Indent
(icon)	Increase Indent

3. Assign a size by clicking the down-arrow beside the Font Size drop-down list and choosing the size; alternatively, you can enter a size in the Font Size text box.

4. To choose a color, click the Font Color tool button and select a color from the palette box that appears.

5. Choose a type style to apply to text by clicking the Bold, Italic, or Underline button (or a combination of them) on the Formatting toolbar.

6. Choose an alignment by selecting the Align Left, Center, or Align Right button from the Formatting toolbar.

7. Add bullets to a list by clicking the Bullet button on the Formatting toolbar.

8. Create text indents or remove indents in half-inch increments by clicking the Increase Indent or Decrease Indent buttons. (Each time you click the Indent button, the indent changes by half an inch.)

CHECKING SPELLING

To make a good impression and to maintain your professional image, you should check the spelling in your mail messages before you send them. Outlook includes a spelling checker you can use for that purpose. And built into that spelling checker is a grammar checker that automatically checks the grammar in your message.

To check the spelling in a message, follow these steps:

1. In the open message, choose Tools, Spelling and Grammar or press F7. When the spelling checker finds a word whose spelling it questions, it displays the Spelling dialog box shown in Figure 8.3). If the checker does not find any misspelled words, a dialog box appears, saying the spelling and grammar check is complete; click OK to close the dialog box.

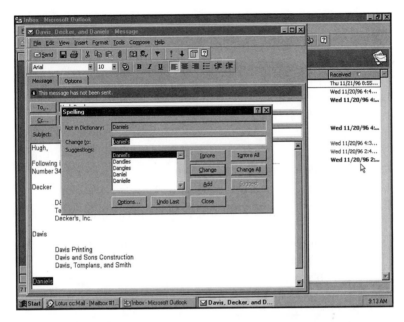

FIGURE 8.3   Check your spelling before sending a message.

2. You can do any of the following in response to the word Outlook questions in the Spelling dialog box:

Not in Dictionary   Enter the correct spelling in this text box.

Suggestions   Select the correct spelling in this text box, and it automatically appears in the Change To text box.

Ignore   Click this button to continue the spelling check without changing this occurrence of the selected word.

Ignore All   Click this button to continue the spelling check without changing any occurrence of the word in question throughout this message.

Change   Click this button to change this particular occurrence of the word in question to the spelling in the Change To text box.

Change All   Click this button to change the word in question to the spelling listed in the Change To text box every time the spelling checker finds the word in this message.

Add   Click this button to add the current spelling of the word in question to the dictionary so that Outlook will not question future occurrences of this spelling.

Undo Last   Click this button to reverse the last spelling change you made, thus returning the word to its original spelling.

Cancel   Click this button to quit the spelling check.

3. When the spelling check is complete, Outlook displays a message box telling you it's done. Click OK to close the dialog box.

 Set Your Spelling Options   Click the Options button in the Spelling dialog box to set options that tell Outlook to do such things as ignore words with numbers, ignore original message text in forwarded messages or replies, always check spelling before sending, and so on.

Sending Mail

When you're ready to send your mail message, do one of the following:

- Click the Send button.

- Choose File, Send.

- Press Ctrl+Enter.

AutoSignature Choose Tools, AutoSignature to have Outlook automatically add a message, quotation, or other text at the end of every message you send. Additionally, after you create an autosignature, you can quickly add it to any message by choosing Insert, AutoSignature.

 Using Windows NT 4.0? You'll need to check your rights and permissions in relation to sending e-mail within your network. Ask your system adminstrator for more information.

In this lesson, you learned to compose a message, format text, check your spelling, and send mail. In the next lesson, you'll learn to set mail options and how to tell if the recipient has received your message.

9

SETTING MAIL OPTIONS

In this lesson, you learn to set options for messages and delivery, and for tracking messages.

CUSTOMIZING OPTIONS

Outlook provides options that enable you to mark any message with priority status so that the recipient knows you need a quick response, or with a sensitivity rating so your words cannot be changed by anyone after the message is sent. With other available options, you can enable the recipients of your message to vote on an issue by including voting buttons in your message and having the replies sent to a specific location.

You also can set delivery options. For example, you can schedule the delivery of a message for a specified delivery time or date if you don't want to send it right now.

To set message options open the Untitled - Message window and click the Options tab. As you can see in Figure 9.1, the options on this tab are separated into four areas. The next four subsections discuss each of the groups of options in detail.

GENERAL OPTIONS

In the General Options area, set any of the following options for your message:

- Click the Importance drop-down arrow and choose a priority level of Low, Normal, or High from the list. (Alternatively, you could click the Importance High or Importance Low tool button on the toolbar.) If you don't specify the level of importance, the message is given Normal Importance.

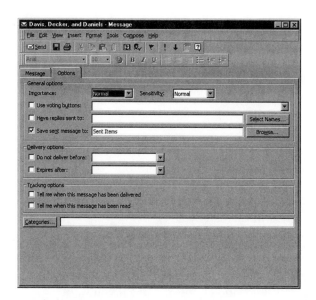

FIGURE 9.1 Use the Options tab to govern how your message is sent.

- Click the Sensitivity drop-down arrow and choose one of the following options:

  Normal   Use this option to indicate that the message's contents are standard or customary.

  Personal   Use this option to suggest that the message's contents are of a personal nature.

  Private   Use this option to prevent the message from being modified after you send it.

  Confidential   Use this option to denote that the message's contents are restricted or private.

You Can Mark All Messages As Private   You can mark all of your messages so that no one can tamper with your words by choosing Tools, Options and clicking the Sending tab. In the Set Sensitivity box, choose the level you want.

- Select the Use Voting Buttons check box to add the default choices (Approve and Reject) to your message. You can also add Yes and No choices or Yes, No, and Maybe choices. If you want to provide other choices, enter your own text in the text box.

- Choose the Have Replies Sent To check box and specify in the text box the person to whom you want the replies sent. You can use the Select Names button to view the Address Book and choose a name if you want.

- Select the Save Sent Message To check box to save your message to the Sent Items folder by default. Or specify another folder to save the message in, using the Browse button and the resulting dialog box if necessary to locate the folder.

DELIVERY OPTIONS

In addition to message options, you can set certain delivery options, such as scheduling the time of the delivery. In the Delivery Options area of the Options tab (Message window), choose one or both of the following check boxes:

Do Not Deliver Before   Check this option to specify a delivery date. Click the down arrow in the text box beside the option to display a calendar on which you can select the day.

Expires After   Select this check box to include a day, date, and time of expiration. You can click the down arrow in the text box to display a calendar from which you can choose a date, or you can enter the date and time yourself.

TRACKING OPTIONS

You might want to set tracking options so you'll know when the message has been delivered and/or read. Tracking options are like receipts: they notify you that the message arrived safely. You set tracking options from the Options tab of the Untitled - Message window.

Choose one or both of the following Tracking Options: Tell Me When This Message Has Been Delivered and Tell Me When This Message Has Been Read.

CATEGORIES

Outlook enables you to assign messages to certain categories—such as Business, Goals, Hot Contacts, Phone Calls, and so on. You set the category for a message in the Categories dialog box.

 Categories   Categories offer a way of organizing messages to make them easier to find, sort, print, and manage. For example, to find all of the items in one category, choose Tools, Find Items. Click the More Choices tab, choose Categories, and check the category for which you're searching.

To assign a category, follow these steps:

1. In the Options tab of the Message window, click the Categories button. The Categories dialog box appears (see Figure 9.2).

2. To assign an existing category, select the category or categories that best suit your message from the Available Categories list. To assign a new category, enter a new category in the Item(s) Belong to These Categories text box, and then click the Add to List button.

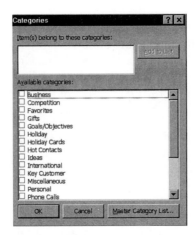

Figure 9.2 Organize your messages with categories.

3. Click OK to close the Categories dialog box and return to the Message window.

Using Message Flags

A message flag enables you to mark a message as important, either as a reminder for yourself or as a signal to the message's recipient. When you send a message flag, a red flag icon appears in the recipient's message list, and Outlook adds text at the top of the message telling which type of flag you are sending. In addition, you can add a due date to the flag, and that date appears at the top of the message.

The following list outlines the types of flags you can send in Outlook:

Call	No Response Necessary
Do not Forward	Read
Follow Up	Reply
For Your Information	Reply to All
Forward	Review

To use a message flag, follow these steps:

1. In the Message window, click the Message Flag button or choose Edit, Message Flag. The Flag Message dialog box appears (see Figure 9.3).

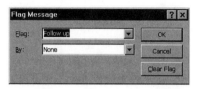

Figure 9.3 Flag a message to show its importance.

2. Click the Flag drop-down arrow and choose the flag text you want to add to the message.

3. Click the By drop-down arrow and select a date from the calendar, or enter a date manually in the text box.

4. Click OK to return to the Message window.

 View the Message Header You can view just the header of a message to allow you more message text room, if you want to hide the Cc, Bcc, and Subject lines. Choose View, Message Header to show only the To text box and any flag text; select View, Message Header again to redisplay the Cc, Bcc, and Subject fields.

In this lesson, you learned to set options for messages and delivery, and for tracking messages. In the next lesson, you will learn to attach items to messages.

10 — ATTACHING ITEMS TO A MESSAGE

*In this lesson, you learn to attach a file, an object (such as an embed-
ded file), and other items (such as an appointment or task)
to a message.*

ATTACHING A FILE

You can attach any type of file to an Outlook message, which
makes for a convenient way of sending your files over the network to your coworkers. You might send Word documents, Excel
spreadsheets, a PowerPoint presentation, or any other document
you create with your Windows 95 applications.

When you send an attached file, it appears as an icon in the message. When the recipient gets the file, he or she can open it
within the message or save it for later use. However, the recipient
must have the source program that you used to create the file on
his or her computer. For instance, if you send a colleague a
Microsoft Word file, he must have Microsoft Word in order to
view the file he receives.

To attach a file to a message, follow these steps:

1. In the Message window, position the insertion point in
   the message text, and then choose Insert, File or click the
   Insert File toolbar button. The Insert File dialog box appears (see Figure 10.1).

2. From the Look In list, choose the drive and folder that
   contains the file you want to attach.

3. Using the Files of Type drop-down list, choose the file
   type—such as Excel or Word.

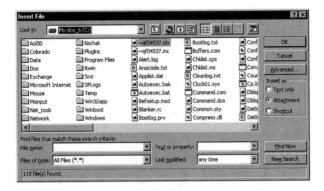

FIGURE 10.1 Select the file you want to attach to a message.

4. Select the file you want to attach.

5. Click OK to insert the file into the message. Figure 10.2 shows a file inserted as an attachment.

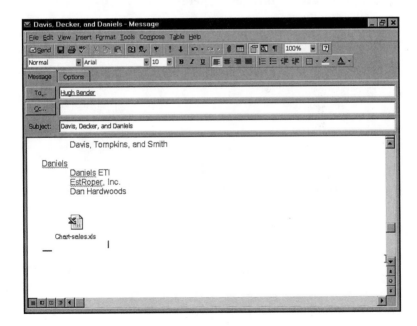

FIGURE 10.2 The recipient can double-click the icon to open the file.

ATTACHING OUTLOOK ITEMS

In addition to attaching files from other programs, you can also attach an Outlook item to a message. An Outlook item can be any document saved in one of your personal folders, including a calendar, contacts, journal, notes, tasks, and so on. You can attach an Outlook item in the same manner you attach a file.

Follow these steps to attach an Outlook item:

1. In the Message window, choose Insert, Item. The Insert Item dialog box appears.

2. From the Look In list, choose the folder containing the item you want to include in the message.

3. Select from the items that appear in the Items list (see Figure 10.3). To select multiple adjacent items, hold the Shift key and click the first and last desired items; to select multiple nonadjacent items, hold the Ctrl key and click the items.

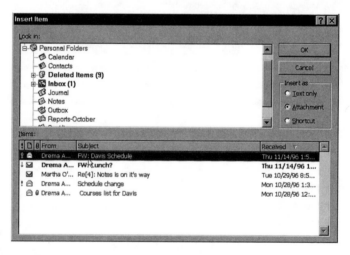

FIGURE 10.3   Select items from any folder in Outlook.

4. In the Insert As area, choose from the following option buttons:

Text Only   Inserts the file as text into the message; if your file is not saved as an ASCII or other text-only file, do not use this option.

Attachment   Inserts an icon representing the document. The actual file follows the message to the recipient, and the recipient saves it as his or her own copy.

Shortcut   Inserts a Windows 95 shortcut icon into the text. This option is best used only if the file is stored on a network drive from which the recipient can easily access it through a shortcut.

Text Only Is Only for Text!   If you try to insert a file from Word, Excel, or another application as Text Only, you'll end up with a lot of "garbage" characters in the text. The only time you will use Text Only is when you export the data from its native program into a text-only file first.

5. Click OK, and Outlook inserts the items in your message.

It Doesn't Work Without Outlook   If the recipient doesn't have Outlook on his computer, he will not be able to view the attached item.

INSERTING AN OBJECT

Just as you can insert an object—a spreadsheet, chart, drawing, presentation, media clip, clip art, WordArt, and so on—in any Windows application that supports *OLE*, you can also insert an object into an Outlook mail message.

You can insert an existing object into a message, or you can create an object within a message using the source application. For example, you could create an Excel chart within your message using Excel's features through OLE.

OLE (Object Linking and Embedding) A method of exchanging data between applications; most Windows applications and all Microsoft programs support OLE.

When you send a message with an attached object, the object travels with the message to the recipient. As long as the recipient has the application on his computer, he can open the object and view it.

To attach an existing object to a message, follow these steps:

1. In the Message window, position the insertion point in the message text and choose Insert, Object. The Object dialog box appears.

2. Choose the Create from File tab (see Figure 10.4).

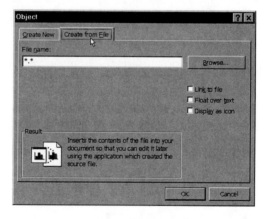

FIGURE 10.4 Insert an object to send with a message.

3. In the File Name text box, enter the path and the name of the file you want to insert. (Or you can use the Browse button and the resulting dialog box to find the file.)

4. Click OK. Outlook inserts the object into the message.

After you save and open an object you've received in a message, you can resize the object to suit your needs. First select it, and a frame appears with eight small black boxes (called *handles*) on the corners and along the sides. To resize the object, position the mouse pointer over one of the black handles; the mouse pointer becomes a two-headed arrow. Click and drag the handle to resize the object.

To edit an object, double-click within the frame, and the source application opens from within Outlook. Note that you'll see some Excel tools and menus you can use to edit the object. Figure 10.5 shows an Excel chart object. Notice the Chart menu and several chart icons added through OLE for use in editing.

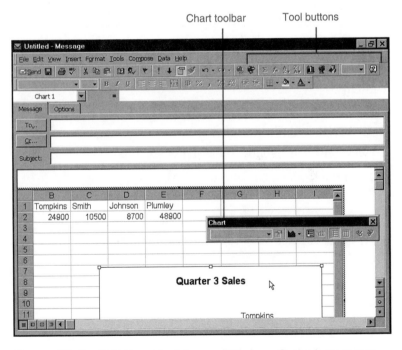

FIGURE 10.5   Edit the object from within your Outlook message.

In this lesson, you learned to attach a file, an object, and other items to a message. In the next lesson, you will learn to organize messages.

ORGANIZING MESSAGES

In this lesson, you learn to view sent items, create folders, and move items to a new folder.

VIEWING SENT ITEMS AND CHANGING DEFAULTS

By default, Outlook saves a copy of all mail messages you send. It keeps these copies in the Sent Items folder, which is part of the Mail group of the Outlook Bar. You can view a list of sent items at any time, and you can open any message in that list to review its contents.

VIEWING SENT ITEMS

To view sent items, follow these steps:

1. In the Outlook Bar, choose the Mail group.

 Save time You can select the Sent Items folder from the Folder List instead of following steps 1–3.

2. If necessary, scroll to the Sent Items folder.

3. Click the Sent Items icon, and Outlook displays a list of the contents of that folder. Figure 11.1 shows the Sent Items list. All messages you send remain in the Sent Items folder until you delete or move them.

4. (Optional) To view a sent item, double-click it to open it. When you finish with it, click the Close (X) button.

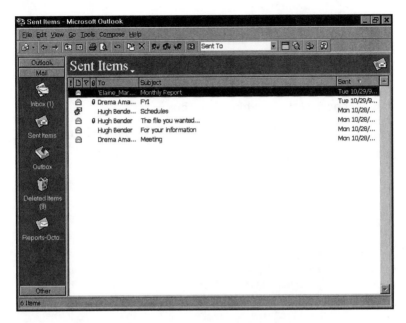

FIGURE 11.1   You can open any sent message by double-clicking it.

CHANGING SENT ITEMS DEFAULTS

You can control how Outlook saves copies of your sent messages. To change the default settings for the Sent Items folder, follow these steps:

1. Choose Tools, Options, and the Options dialog box appears.

2. Click the Sending tab.

3. Choose one or all of the following options (located near the bottom of the dialog box):

   Save Copies of Messages in "Sent Items" Folder   When this is checked, Outlook saves copies of all sent messages to the specified folder. (When the check box is empty, no copies of messages are saved automatically.)

In Folders Other Than the Inbox, Save Replies with Original Messages   When this is checked, Outlook saves replies to messages in the same folder in which you store the original message. (When the check box is empty, it saves replies to the Sent Items folder as long as you've checked the previous check box.)

Save Forwarded Messages   When this is checked, Outlook saves a copy of each forwarded message you send.

4. Click OK to close the dialog box.

Too Much Mail!   If you save all the mail you receive and send, you may accumulate so much mail that you run the risk of running out of disk space. You can and should periodically delete mail from the Sent Items folder by selecting the mail and pressing the Delete key; you'll also need to remove the deleted mail from the Deleted Items folder. See Lesson 6, "Managing Mail," for more information. Alternatively, you can create an archive file of the messages you've sent. The archive enables you to save items on disk or elsewhere on the system. See Lesson 22, "Archiving Items," for details.

CREATING FOLDERS

You'll likely want to organize your mail in various folders to make storing items and finding them more efficient. You can create folders within Outlook that make it easier to manage your mail and other items in Outlook.

To create a folder, follow these steps:

1. Choose File, Folder, Create Subfolder. **The Create New Folder dialog box appears (see Figure 11.2).**

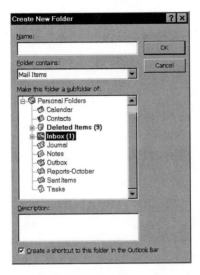

FIGURE 11.2   Create folders to organize your mail and other items.

2. In the Name text box, enter a name for the folder.

3. Click the Folder Contains drop-down arrow, and choose the type of items the folder will store: Mail, Appointments, Contact, Journal, Note, or Task.

4. In the Make This Folder a Subfolder Of list, choose the folder in which you want to create the new folder. You can, for example, make the new folder a subfolder of Personal Folders so that it appears in lists with all of the Outlook folders. Or you might want to make it a subfolder of Sent Mail.

5. (Optional) In the Description text box, add a comment or brief description of the folder.

6. (Optional) Click the Create a Shortcut to This Folder in the Outlook Bar check box to remove the check mark if you prefer not to see the folder in the Outlook Bar. (By default, the check box is checked so that you will see the new folder in the Outlook Bar.)

7. Click OK to close the dialog box. The new folder appears on the Outlook Bar and in the Folder List.

Add Folder Later Even if you choose not to add the folder to the Outlook Bar when you create the folder, you can add it later. You simply choose File, Add to Outlook Bar. In the dialog box that appears, you can select any folder name in Outlook or on the system and add it to the Outlook Bar by selecting it and clicking OK.

I Want to Delete a Folder! If you added a folder by accident or you change your mind about a folder you've added, you can delete it from Outlook. To delete a folder, select it and then choose File, Folder, Delete *foldername*. You also can rename, move, and/or copy the folder using the commands in the secondary menu that appears when you choose File, Folder.

MOVING ITEMS TO ANOTHER FOLDER

You can move items from one folder in Outlook to another; for example, you may create a folder to store all messages pertaining to a specific account or report. You can easily move those messages to the new folder and open them later for reference purposes. You also can forward, reply, copy, delete, and archive any items you move from one folder to another.

To move an item to another folder, follow these steps:

1. From the Inbox or any Outlook folder, open the message you want to move.

2. Choose File, Move to Folder. The Move Item to dailog box appears (see Figure 11.3).

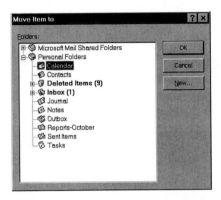

FIGURE 11.3   Choose the folder in which you want to store the message.

3. In the list of folders, select the folder to which you want to move the message.

4. Click OK. When you close the message, Outlook stores it in the designated folder.

 Quick Move   You can quickly move an unopened message by dragging it from the open folder in which it resides to any folder icon in the Outlook Bar.

You can open the message at any time by opening the folder from the Outlook bar and double-clicking the message. After opening it, you can forward, send, print, or otherwise manipulate the message as you would any other.

In this lesson, you learned to save a draft, view sent items, and create folders. In the next lesson, you'll learn to use the Calendar.

12 USING THE CALENDAR

In this lesson, you learn to navigate the Calendar, create appointments, and save appointments.

NAVIGATING THE CALENDAR

You can use Outlook's Calendar to schedule appointments and create a to-do list, if necessary, to remind you of daily or weekly tasks. You can schedule appointments months in advance, move appointments, cancel appointments, and so on. And the Calendar makes it easy to identify days on which you have appointments.

To open the Outlook Calendar, click the Calendar icon in the Outlook Bar or select the Calendar folder from the Folder List. Figure 12.1 shows the Calendar in Outlook.

Outlook provides multiple ways for you to move around in the Calendar and view specific dates:

- Scroll through the schedule pane to view the time of the appointment.

- In the monthly calendar pane, click the left and right arrows next to the names of the months to go backward and forward one month at a time.

- In the monthly calendar pane, click a date to display that date in the schedule pane.

- To view a full month in the schedule pane, select the name of the month in the monthly calendar pane.

- To view a week or selected days in the schedule pane, select the days in the monthly calendar pane.

- To add a task to the Task list, click where you see **Click here to add a new Task**.

- Use the scroll bars for the Task list pane to view appointments, if necessary.

Change the Date Quickly To quickly go to today's date or to a specific date without searching through the monthly calendar pane, right-click in the schedule pane and choose either Go To Today or Go To Date.

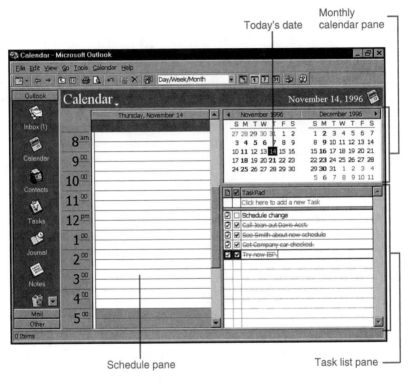

Figure 12.1 You can view all appointments and tasks.

CREATING AN APPOINTMENT

You can create an appointment on any day well past the year 2000 using the Outlook Calendar. When you create an appointment, you can add the subject, location, starting time, category, and even an alarm to remind you ahead of time. Follow these steps to create an appointment:

1. In the monthly calendar pane, select the month and the date for which you want to create an appointment.

2. In the schedule pane, double-click next to the time at which the appointment is scheduled to begin. The Untitled - Appointment dialog box appears, with the Appointment tab displayed (see Figure 12.2).

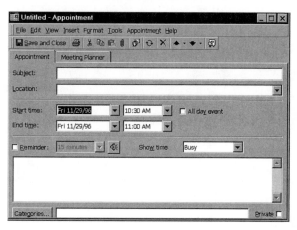

Figure 12.2   Enter all the details you need when scheduling an appointment.

3. Enter the subject of the appointment in the Subject text box (you can use a person's name, a topic, or other information).

4. In the Location text box, enter the meeting place or other text that will help you identify the meeting when you see it in your calendar.

5. Enter dates and times in the Start Time and End Time text boxes (or click the drop-down arrows and select the dates and times).

TIP   **Autodate It!**   You can use Outlook's Autodate feature: enter a text phrase such as "next Friday" or "noon" in the date and time text boxes, and Outlook figures out the date for you.

6. Select the Reminder check box and enter the amount of time before the appointment that you want to be notified. If you want to set an audio alarm, click the alarm bell button and select a specific sound for Outlook to play as your reminder.

7. From the Show Time As drop-down list, choose how you want to display the scheduled time on your calendar.

8. In the large text box near the bottom of the Appointment tab, enter any text that you want to include, such as text to identify the appointment, reminders for materials to take, and so on.

9. Click the Categories button and assign a category to the appointment.

10. Click the Save and Close button to return to the calendar.

The Meeting Planner tab enables you to schedule a meeting with coworkers and enter the meeting on your Calendar. See Lesson 13 for more information.

SCHEDULING A RECURRING APPOINTMENT

Suppose you have an appointment that comes around every week or month, or that otherwise occurs on a regular basis. Instead of scheduling every individual occurrence of the appointment, you can schedule that appointment in your calendar as a recurring appointment.

To schedule a recurring appointment, follow these steps:

1. In the Calendar folder, choose Calendar, New Recurring Appointment. The Appointment dialog box appears, and then the Appointment Recurrence dialog box appears (as shown in Figure 12.3).

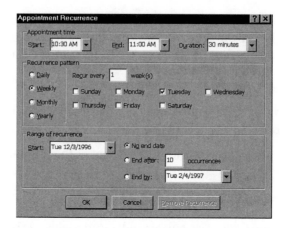

Figure 12.3 Schedule a recurring appointment once, and Outlook fills in the appointment for you throughout the Calendar.

2. In the Appointment Time area, enter the Start, End, and Duration times for the appointment.

3. In the Recurrence Pattern area, indicate the frequency of the appointment: Daily, Weekly, Monthly, or Yearly. After you select one of these options, the rest of the Recurrence Pattern area changes.

4. Enter the day and month, as well as any other options in the Recurrence Pattern area that are specific to your selection in step 3.

5. In the Range of Recurrence area, enter appropriate time limits according to these guidelines:

> Start   Choose the date on which the recurring appointments will begin.
>
> No End Date   Choose this option if the recurring appointments are not on a limited schedule.
>
> End After   Choose this option and enter the number of appointments if there is a specific limit to the recurring appointments.
>
> End By   Choose this option and enter an ending date to limit the number of recurring appointments.

6. Click OK to close the Appointment Recurrence dialog box. The Appointment dialog box appears.

7. Fill in the Appointment dialog box as described previously in this lesson. When you finish, click the Save and Close button to return to the Calendar. The recurring appointment appears in your calendar on the specified date and time. A recurring appointment contains a double arrow icon to indicate that it is recurring.

Planning Events

In the Outlook Calendar, an *event* is any activity that lasts at least 24 hours, such as a trade show or a conference. You can plan an event in the Calendar program to block off larger time slots than you would for normal appointments. In addition, you can schedule recurring events.

To schedule an event, choose Calendar, New Event. The Event dialog box appears; it looks very much like the New Appointment dialog box. Fill in the Subject, Location, Start Time, and End Time text boxes. Make sure the All Day Event check box is checked (that's the only difference between an Event and an Appointment). Click the Save and Close button to return to the Outlook Calendar. The appointment appears in gray at the beginning of the day for which you scheduled the event.

To schedule a recurring event, choose Calendar, New Recurring Event. Fill in the Appointment Recurrence dialog box as you learned to in the previous section. When you close the Appointment Recurrence dialog box, the Recurring Event dialog box appears. Fill it in as you would the Event dialog box. Then click the Save and Close button.

To edit an event or a recurring event, double-click the event in your calendar. As with a mail message or appointment, Outlook opens the event window so you can change times, dates, or other details of the event.

In this lesson, you learned to navigate the Calendar, create appointments, and save appointments. In the next lesson, you will learn to plan a meeting.

PLANNING A MEETING

In this lesson, you learn to schedule a meeting, enter attendees for a planned meeting, set the meeting date and time, and invite others to the meeting.

SCHEDULING A MEETING

Outlook provides a method by which you can plan the time and date of a meeting, identify the subject and location of the meeting, and invite others to attend the meeting. You use the Calendar folder to plan and schedule meetings.

Meeting   In Outlook, a meeting is an appointment to which you invite people and resources.

Attendees   The people who will be attending your meeting.

Resources   Any equipment you use in your meeting, such as a computer, slide projector, or even the room itself.

To plan a meeting, follow these steps:

1. Click the icon for the Calendar folder, and then choose Calendar, Plan a Meeting. The Plan a Meeting dialog box appears (see Figure 13.1).

2. To enter the names of the attendees, click in the All Attendees list where it says **Type Attendee Name Here**. Enter the name and press Enter. Continue adding new names as necessary.

Green bar is   Red bar is
starting time.   ending time.

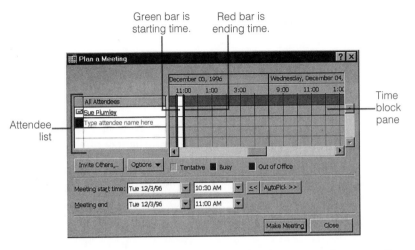

FIGURE 13.1 Choose the date and time of your meeting as well as the attendees.

Invite More People You can click the Invite Others button to choose names from your Personal Address Book or the Outlook Address Book.

3. To set a date for the meeting, open the leftmost Meeting Start Time drop-down list and select the date from the calendar, or just type the date in the text box. The ending date (in the Meeting End Time drop-down list) automatically shows the same date you set in the Meeting Start Time date box; you can change the End Time date if you want.

4. To set a start time for the meeting, do one of the following:

   • Open the rightmost Meeting Start Time drop-down list and select the time.

   • Type a time in the text box.

   • Drag the green bar in the time block pane of the dialog box to set the start time.

5. To set an end time for the meeting, do one of the following:

   • Open the rightmost Meeting End Time drop-down list and select the end time.

   • Type a time in the text box.

   • Drag the red bar in the time block pane of the dialog box to change the ending time of the meeting.

6. When you finish planning the meeting, click the Make Meeting button. The Meeting window appears (see Figure 13.2), from which you can refine the meeting details, as described in the next section.

WORKING OUT MEETING DETAILS

After you plan a meeting, Outlook enables you to send invitations, identify the subject of the meeting, and specify the meeting's location. You enter these details in the Meeting dialog box.

When you schedule a meeting (as described in the previous section) you finish by clicking the Make Meeting button in the Plan a Meeting dialog box. When you do that, Outlook displays the Meeting dialog box with the Appointment tab in front (see Figure 13.2).

Follow these steps to specify meeting details for a meeting you've already scheduled.

1. If you did not list the attendees in the Plan a Meeting dialog box, either click in the To text box and enter the names of the people you want to attend the meeting, or click the To button to select the attendees from an address book.

2. In the Subject text box, enter a subject for the meeting.

3. In the Location text box, enter a location for the meeting.

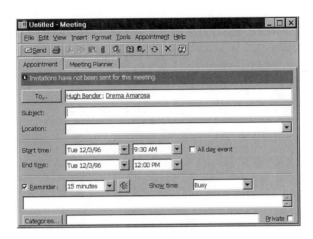

FIGURE 13.2 Specify the details about the meeting in the Appointment tab of the Meeting dialog box.

4. (Optional) You can change the starting and ending dates and/or times in the Appointment tab. You can also choose the Meeting Planner tab to view the meeting in a format similar to that of the Plan a Meeting dialog box; make any changes to attendees, time, dates, and so on in the Meeting Planner tab.

5. (Optional) Select the Reminder check box and enter a time for Outlook to sound an alarm to remind you of the meeting.

6. (Optional) Enter any special text you want to send the attendees in the text box provided.

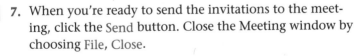 7. When you're ready to send the invitations to the meeting, click the Send button. Close the Meeting window by choosing File, Close.

When you send an invitation, you're sending an e-mail that requests the presence of the recipient at the meeting. The recipient can reply to your message, save your message, and forward or delete the message, just as he can with any other e-mail message. If you want the recipient to reply, choose Appointment, Request Responses, and the recipients will be prompted to reply to your invitation.

An Invitation Mistake   To cancel an invitation after you've sent it, choose Appointment, Cancel Invitation.

INVITING OTHERS TO THE MEETING

If you need to add names to your attendees list—either while you're planning the meeting or at some later date—you can use your personal address book and/or the Outlook address book to find the names of the people you want to invite. Additionally, you can choose whether to make the meeting required or optional for each person you invite.

To invite others to the meeting, follow these steps:

1. In either the Plan a Meeting dialog box or the Meeting Planner tab of the Meeting dialog box, click the Invite Others button. The Select Attendees and Resources dialog box appears, as shown in Figure 13.3.

2. Open the Show Names from The drop-down list and choose either Personal Address Book or Outlook Address Book.

3. To add a new name to a list, click the New button, and then enter the name, e-mail address, phone numbers, and other pertinent information about the name you're adding to the list.

4. Select any name in the list on the left side of the dialog box and click the Required or Optional button to specify attendance requirements.

5. Click OK to close the dialog box and add any attendees to your list.

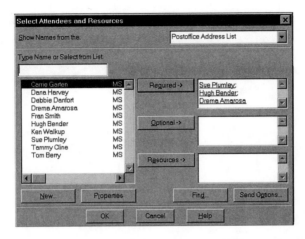

FIGURE 13.3   Use the address books to specify attendees to your meeting.

TIP   **Reserve Resources**   Click the New button to add resources to the list; then notify the person who is in charge of those resources of your meeting.

EDITING A MEETING

You can edit the details about a meeting, invite additional people, or change the date and time of the meeting at any time by opening the Meeting dialog box.

To open the Meeting dialog box and edit the meeting, follow these steps:

1. In the Calendar folder, choose the meeting date in the monthly calendar pane. The date appears in the schedule pane, and the meeting is blocked out for the time period you specified, as shown in Figure 13.4.

2. Double-click the meeting block to display the Meeting dialog box. You can edit anything in the Appointment or Meeting Planner tabs.

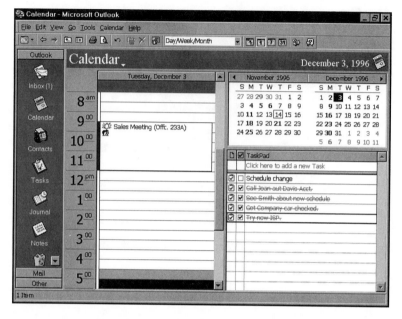

FIGURE 13.4 Select the meeting you want to edit from within the Calendar.

 TIP **Any Responses?** Choose the Show Attendee Status option in the Meeting Planner tab of the Meeting dialog box to see if the people you invited to the meeting have responded to your invitation.

3. When you're done, choose File Close to close the Meeting dialog box. If you've made changes to the meet-ing specifics, you should also send a message to your attendees to notify them of the change.

In this lesson, you learned to schedule a meeting, enter attendees for a planned meeting, set the meeting time, and invite others to the meeting. In the next lesson, you'll learn to create a contacts list.

CREATING A CONTACTS LIST

*In this lesson, you learn to create
and view a Contacts list, and to send mail to someone
on your Contacts list.*

CREATING A NEW CONTACT

You use the Contacts folder to create, store, and utilize your Contacts list. You can enter any or all of the following information about each contact:

- Name
- Job title
- Company name
- Address (Street, City, State, ZIP, Country)
- Phone (business, home, business fax, mobile)
- E-mail address
- Web page address
- Comments, notes, or descriptions
- Categories

Contact In Outlook, a contact is any person or company for which you've entered a name, address, phone number, or other information. You can communicate with a contact in Outlook by sending an e-mail message, scheduling a meeting, sending a letter, and so on.

You also can edit the information at any time, add new contacts, or delete contacts from the list. To create a new contact, follow these steps:

1. Click the Contacts button or choose the Contacts folder. If you haven't used the list before, the folder is empty.

2. Choose Contacts, New Contact, or simply click the New Contact button on the Toolbar. The Contact dialog box appears, with the General tab displayed (see Figure 14.1).

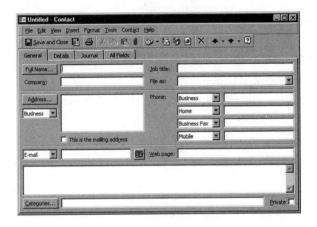

FIGURE 14.1   You can enter as much or as little information about each contact as you need.

3. Click the Full Name button to display the Check Full Name dialog box, and then enter the contact's title and full name (including first, middle, and last names) and any suffix you want to include. Alternatively, you can enter the name in the text box.

4. (Optional) Enter the client's company name and job title.

5. In the File As drop-down box, enter or select the method by which you want to file your contact's names. You can choose last name first or first name first, or you can enter your own filing system, such as by company or state.

Keep It Simple   The default filing method for contacts is last name first, which makes it easy to quickly find the contact when you need it.

6. (Optional) Enter the address in the Address box and choose whether the address is Business, Home, or Other. Alternatively, you can click the Address button to enter the street, city, state, ZIP code, and country in specified areas instead of all within the text block. You can add a second address (say, the home address) if you want.

7. In the Phone drop-down lists, choose the type of phone number—Business, Callback, Car, Home Fax, ISDN, Pager, and so on—and then enter the number. You can enter up to 19 numbers in each of the four drop-down boxes in the Phone area of the dialog box.

8. (Optional) Enter up to three e-mail addresses in the E-mail text box; in the Web Page text box, enter the address for the company or contact's WWW page.

9. (Optional) In the comment text box, enter any descriptions, comments, or other pertinent information. Then select or enter a category to classify the contact.

10. Open the File menu and choose one of the following commands:

   Save   Saves the record and closes the dialog box.

   Save and New   Saves the record and clears the Contact dialog box so you can enter a new contact.

   Save and New in Company   Saves the record and clears the Name, Job Title, File As, E-Mail, and comment text boxes so you can enter a new contact within the same company.

You can edit the information about a contact at any time by double-clicking the contact's name in the Contacts list; this displays the contact's information window. Alternatively, you can click within the information listed below a contact's name (such as the phone number or address) to position the insertion point in the text, and then delete or enter text. Press Enter to complete the modifications you've made and move to the next contact in the list.

VIEWING THE CONTACTS LIST

By default, you see the contacts in an Address Cards view. The information you see displays the contact's name and other data such as addresses and phone numbers. The contact's company name, job title, and comments, however, are not displayed by default. Figure 14.2 shows the Contacts list in the default Address Cards view.

Change views here.

Quickly find a contact using the index.

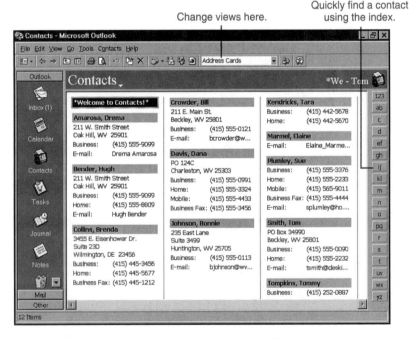

FIGURE 14.2 View your contacts in Address Cards view.

You can use the horizontal scroll bar to view more contacts, or you can click a letter in the index to display contacts beginning with that letter in the first column of the list.

Do I Save View Settings?   Depending on the changes you make to a view, Outlook might display the Save View Settings dialog box to ask if you want to save the view settings before you switch to a different view. If you choose to save the current settings, Outlook lets you name the view and adds that view to the Current View list. If you choose to discard the current settings, your modifications to the view will be lost. If you choose to update the view, your modifications are saved with that view.

You can change how you view the contacts in the list by choosing one of these options from the Current View drop-down list on the Standard toolbar:

Address Cards   Displays File As names (last name first, first name last, and so on), addresses, and phone numbers of the contacts, depending on the amount of information you've entered in a card format.

Detailed Address Cards   Displays File As name, full name, job title, company, addresses, phone numbers, e-mail addresses, categories, and comments in a card format.

Phone List   Displays full name, job title, company, File As name, department, phone numbers, and categories in a table, organizing each entry horizontally in rows and columns.

By Category   Displays contacts in rows by categories. The information displayed is the same as what's displayed in a phone list.

By Company   Displays contacts in rows, grouped by their company. The information displayed is the same as what's displayed in a phone list.

By Location   Displays contacts grouped by country. The information displayed is the same as what's displayed in a phone list.

COMMUNICATING WITH A CONTACT

You can send messages to any of your contacts, arrange meetings, assign tasks, or even send a letter to a contact from within Outlook. To communicate with a contact, make sure you're in the Contacts folder. You do not need to open the specific contact's information window to perform any of the following procedures.

SENDING MESSAGES

To send a message to a contact, you must make sure you have entered an e-mail address in the General tab of the Contact dialog box for that particular contact. If Outlook cannot locate the mailing address, it displays the message dialog box shown in Figure 14.3.

FIGURE 14.3   Outlook cannot send the e-mail until you complete the address in the New Message dialog box.

In the Check Names dialog box, choose one of the following options:

To send a message from the Contacts folder, select the contact and choose Contacts, New Message to Contact. In the Untitled - Message dialog box, enter the subject and message and set any options you want. When you're ready to send the message, click the Send button. For more information about sending mail, see Lesson 8, "Creating Mail."

SCHEDULING A MEETING WITH A CONTACT

To schedule a meeting with a contact, the contact must have a valid e-mail address. If no address is listed for the contact, Outlook notifies you with a message box and enables you to enter an address within the message dialog box. If the listed address is not found, Outlook responds with the Check Names dialog box, as described in the previous section.

To schedule a meeting with a contact, select the contact and choose Contacts, New Meeting with Contact. The Untitled - Meeting dialog box appears. Enter the subject, location, time and date, and other information you need to schedule the meeting, and then notify the contact by sending an invitation. For more information about scheduling meetings, see Lesson 13, "Planning a Meeting."

ASSIGNING A TASK TO A CONTACT

Tasks are assigned through e-mail. Therefore, you must enter a valid e-mail address for the contact before you can assign him or her a task.

To assign a task to a contact, select the contact and choose Contacts, New Task for Contact. The Task dialog box appears. Enter the subject, due date, status, and other information, and then send the task to the contact. For detailed information about assigning tasks, see Lesson 15, "Creating a Task List."

SENDING A LETTER TO A CONTACT

Outlook uses the Microsoft Word Letter Wizard to help you create a letter to send to a contact. Within the Letter Wizard, you follow directions as they appear on-screen to complete the text of the letter.

To send a letter to the contact, select the contact in the Contact folder and choose Contacts, New Letter to Contact. Word opens the Letter Wizard on-screen. The Letter Wizard helps you format and complete the letter (see Figure 14.4). All you have to do is follow the directions and make your choices. You can click the Office Assistant button if you need additional help.

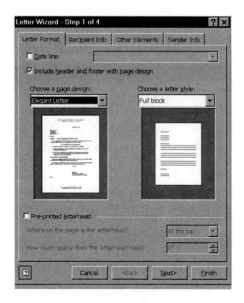

FIGURE 14.4 Use Word's Letter Wizard to create a letter to a contact.

In this lesson, you learned to create a Contacts list, view the list, and send mail to someone on your Contacts list. In the next lesson, you'll learn to create a task list.

CREATING A TASK LIST

In this lesson, you learn to enter a task and record statistics about the task.

ENTERING A TASK

You can use the Task folder to create and manage your task list. You can list due dates, status, and priorities, and even set reminder alarms so you don't forget to perform certain tasks.

> **Task List** A task list is simply a list of things you must do to complete your work, plan for a meeting, arrange an event, and so on. Various tasks might include making a phone call, writing a letter, printing a spreadsheet, or making airline reservations.

To enter a task, follow these steps:

1. In the Tasks folder, choose Tasks, New Task or click the New Task button on the Toolbar. The Untitled - Task dialog box appears (see Figure 15.1).

2. In the Task tab, enter the subject of the task.

3. (Optional) Enter a date on which the task should be complete, or click the down arrow to open the Due drop-down calendar and then choose a due date.

4. (Optional) Enter a start date, or click the down arrow to open the Start drop-down calendar and then choose a starting date.

5. From the Status drop-down list, choose the current status of the project: Not Started, In Progress, Completed, Waiting on Someone Else, or Deferred.

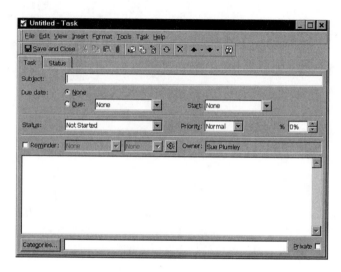

Figure 15.1 Enter data such as due dates, priority, and the subject of the task.

6. In the Priority drop-down list, choose Normal, Low, or High priority.

7. In the % Complete text box, type a percentage or use the spinner arrows to enter one.

8. (Optional) To set an alarm to remind you to start the task or complete the task, select the Reminder check box, and enter a date and a time in the associated text boxes.

9. Enter any comments, descriptions, or other information related to the task in the comments text box.

10. Click the Categories button and choose a category, or simply enter your own category in the text box.

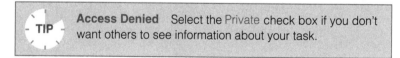

TIP **Access Denied** Select the Private check box if you don't want others to see information about your task.

11. Click Save and Close when you're done.

VIEWING TASKS

As in any Outlook folder, you can change how you view tasks in the list using the Current View drop-down list in the Standard Toolbar. By default, the Tasks folder displays tasks in a Simple List view. Following is a description of the views you can use to display the Tasks folder:

Simple List   Lists the tasks, completed check box, subject, and due date.

Detailed List   Displays the tasks, priority, subject, status, percent complete, and categories.

Active Tasks   Displays the same information as the detailed list but doesn't show any completed tasks.

Next Seven Days   Displays only those tasks you've scheduled for the next seven days, including completed tasks.

Overdue Tasks   Shows a list of tasks that are past due.

By Category   Displays tasks by category; click the button representing the category you want to view.

Assignment   Lists tasks assigned to you by others.

By Person Responsible   Lists tasks grouped by the person who assigned the tasks.

Completed Tasks   Lists only those tasks completed, along with their due dates and completion dates.

Task Timeline   Uses the Timeline view to display tasks by day, week, or month. Figure 15.2 shows the tasks assigned within one week.

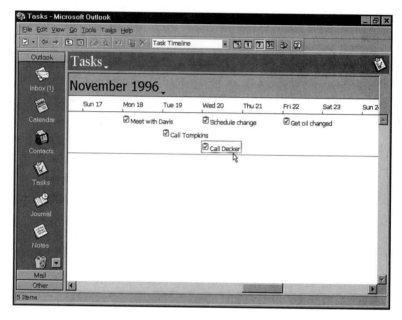

FIGURE 15.2   Double-click a task in Timeline view to edit it.

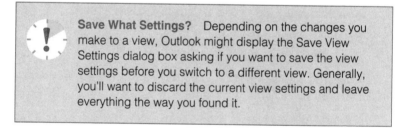

Save What Settings?   Depending on the changes you make to a view, Outlook might display the Save View Settings dialog box asking if you want to save the view settings before you switch to a different view. Generally, you'll want to discard the current view settings and leave everything the way you found it.

MANAGING TASKS

When working with a task list, you can add and delete tasks, mark tasks as completed, and arrange the tasks within the list. You also can perform any of these procedures in most of the task views described in the previous section. For information about printing a task list, see Lesson 18, "Printing in Outlook."

Figure 15.3 shows the Task folder; the following list describes how to manage certain tasks in the list.

Completed task | Check here to complete a task. | Quickly add a new task here. | Click here to sort by subject. | Click here to sort by due date.

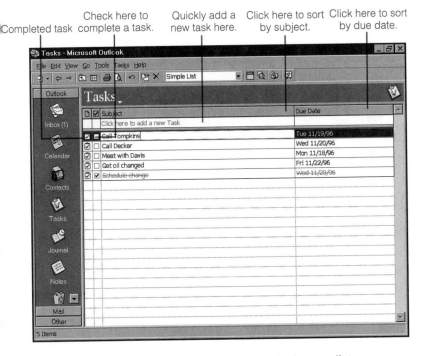

FIGURE 15.3   Add, delete, and sort the tasks in your list.

- To quickly add a task, click the top row of the task list where it says **Click Here to Add a New Task** and enter the subject and date.

- To edit a task, double-click the task in the list. The task dialog box appears.

- To mark a task as completed, click the check box in the second column from the left, or right-click the task and choose Mark Complete from the shortcut menu. Outlook places a line through the task.

- To delete a task, right-click the task and choose Delete from the shortcut menu.

- To assign a task to someone else, right-click the task and choose Assign Task from the shortcut menu. Fill in the name of the person to whom you want to assign the task and click the Send button to e-mail him or her the task request.

- To assign a new task to someone else, choose Tasks, New Task Request. Create the task as you normally would, but send the task as an e-mail by clicking the Send button.

Get Rid of the Default Task   If you don't want to leave the Start up Microsoft Outlook task on your list, you can right-click the task and choose Delete.

Recording Statistics About a Task

You can record statistics about a task, such as time spent completing the task, billable time, contacts, and so on, for your own records or for reference when sharing tasks with your coworkers. This feature is particularly helpful when you assign tasks to others; you can keep track of assigned tasks and find out when the tasks are completed.

To enter statistics about a task, open any task in the task list and click the Status tab. Figure 15.4 shows a completed Status tab for a sample task.

The following list describes the text boxes in the Status tab and the types of information you can enter:

Date Completed   Enter the date the task was completed, or click the arrow to display the calendar and choose the date.

Total Work   Enter the amount of time you expect the task to take. When you complete the job, Outlook calculates the actual time spent and enters it in this text box.

Actual Work   Enter the amount of time it actually took to complete the job.

Mileage   Enter the number of miles you traveled to complete the task.

Billing Information   Enter any specific billing information, such as hours billed, resources used, charges for equipment, and so on.

Contacts   Enter the names of in-house or outside contacts associated with the task. Separate multiple names with semi-colons.

Companies   Enter the names of any companies associated with the contacts or with the project in general.

Update List   Automatically lists the people whose task lists are updated when you make a change to your task.

Create Unassigned Copy   Copies the task so it can be reassigned; use the button to send a task to someone other than an original recipient. If the task is not sent to someone else, the button is unavailable.

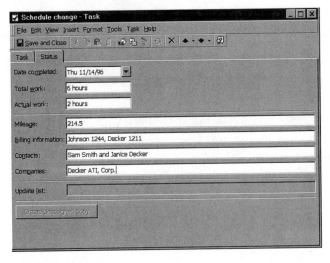

FIGURE 15.4   Fill in the status of the task so you can share it with others and keep personal records.

To track tasks you've assigned to others and to receive status reports, follow these steps:

1. In the Outlook dialog box, choose Tools, Options. The
   Options dialog box appears with the Tasks/Notes tab displayed.

2. In the Task Defaults area of the dialog box, check the
   Keep Updated Copies of Assigned Tasks on My Task List
   check box. This automatically tracks the progress of new
   tasks that you assign to others.

3. Check the Send Status Reports When Assigned Tasks
   are Completed check box to automatically receive
   notification upon the completion of assigned tasks.

4. Click OK to accept the changes and close the dialog box.

Color Your World   You can also set colors to represent
tasks within the Tasks/Notes tab of the Options dialog
box. Outlook offers twenty different colors from which you
can choose for overdue tasks and completed tasks.

In this lesson, you learned to enter a task and record statistics
about the task. In the next lesson, you will learn to use the
Journal.

USING THE JOURNAL

In this lesson, you learn to create journal entries manually and automatically and to change views in the Journal.

CREATING A JOURNAL ENTRY

You can create a record of various items and documents so you can track your work, communications, reports, and so on. In the journal, you can manually record any activities, items, or tasks you want. You also can automatically record e-mail messages, faxes, meeting requests, meeting responses, task requests, and task responses. Additionally, you can automatically record documents created in the other Office applications: Access, Excel, Office Binder, PowerPoint, and Word.

> **Journal** A folder within Outlook that you can use to record interactions, phone calls, message responses, and other activities important to your work.
>
> **Item** An article or object in Outlook, such as a task, appointment, or contact.

You can automatically or manually record items in your journal. You can, for example, choose to automatically record your e-mail messages, meeting requests, task responses, and so on. When you automatically record items in the journal, Outlook records all items you receive. However, if you don't want to record all items, you can have Outlook record only those items you choose by manually adding them to your journal. For example, you might add only the e-mail relating to one account or one client instead of all e-mail you receive.

Manually Recording an Entry

To manually record a journal entry, follow these steps:

1. In the Inbox folder (or any other folder in Outlook), select the item you want to record in the journal and choose Tools, Record in Journal. The Journal Entry dialog box appears (see Figure 16.1).

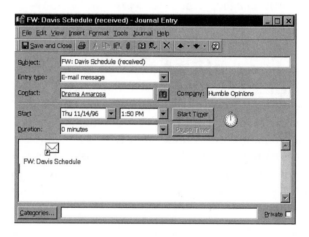

Figure 16.1   Record any Outlook item in the Journal.

2. The Subject, Entry Type, Contact, and Company boxes and other information is entered for you from the selected task, contact, or other selected item. However, you can change any of the statistics you want by entering new information in the following text boxes:

    Subject   Displays the title or name of the item.

    Entry Type   Describes the item based on its point of origin, such as a Word document, Meeting or Appointment, and so on.

    Contact   Lists the name(s) of any attendees, contacts, or other people involved with the selected item.

    Company   Lists the company or companies associated with the contacts.

Start Time   Displays the date and time of the meeting, appointment, or other item.

Start Timer   Like a stop watch, the timer records the time that passes until you click the Pause Timer button.

Pause Timer   Stops the timer.

Duration   The amount of time for completing the item.

Text box   Displays shortcuts to any text, documents, details, or other information related to the item.

Categories   Enter or select a category in which to place the item.

3. Click Save and Close to complete the entry.

TIP   **Time Your Calls**   When making phone calls or meeting with clients, create a journal entry to record the event, and use the Start Timer and Pause Timer buttons to record billable time.

If you want to create a new journal entry, but you don't have a contact, task, e-mail, or other related item for the entry, you can manually record a journal entry by following these steps:

1. Change to the Journal folder.

2. Choose Journal, New Journal Entry or click the New Journal Entry button on the Standard toolbar. The Journal Entry dialog box appears.

3. Enter the subject, entry type, contact, time, and any other information you want to record.

4. When you finish, click Save and Close.

AUTOMATICALLY RECORDING ENTRIES

You can set options to automatically record items and their related contacts and/or statistics about Microsoft Office documents you create. Suppose you want to keep a record, for example, of all memos you send to your boss. You can record it in your journal. To set the options to automatically record journal entries, follow these steps:

1. In the Journal folder, choose Tools, Options. The Options dialog box appears with the Journal tab displayed, as shown in Figure 16.2.

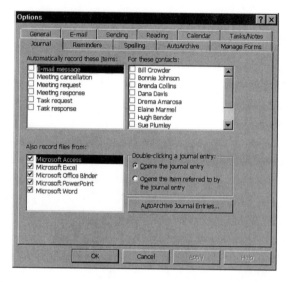

FIGURE 16.2   Set options for automatically recording items.

2. In the Automatically Record These Items list, check those items you want Outlook to automatically record in your journal. (The items recorded correspond with those people selected in the list of contacts in step 3.)

3. In the For These Contacts list, check any contacts you want automatically recorded in the Journal. Outlook records any items checked in step 2 that apply to the selected contacts.

4. In the Also Record Files From list, check the applications for which you want to record journal entries. Outlook

records the date and time you create or modify files in the selected program.

 Automatic and Easy   When you're creating a new contact in Outlook, you can set items to be automatically recorded in the journal by choosing the Journal tab in the Contact dialog box and checking the Automatically Record Journal Entries for This Contact check box.

VIEWING JOURNAL ENTRIES

By default, the Journal folder displays information in the Timeline view and By Type, as shown in Figure 16.3. However, you can display the entries in any of the views described in the following list.

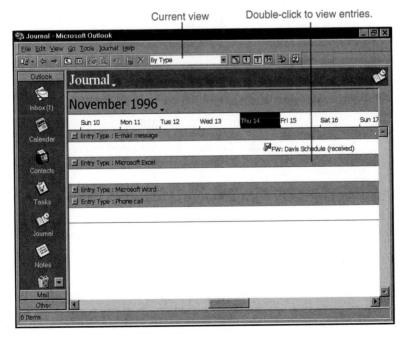

FIGURE 16.3   View the journal entries by type.

Save Settings?   As in other views, Outlook might display the Save View Settings dialog box to ask if you want to save the view settings before you switch to a different view. You're probably getting used to this dialog box by now.

By Type   In Timeline view, this option groups journal entries by type, such as e-mail messages, meetings, Word documents, and so on. Double-click a type to display its contents, and then position the mouse pointer over an entry to view its contents or name.

By Contact   In Timeline view, this displays the name of each contact that you selected in the Options dialog box. Double-click any contact's name to view recorded entries.

By Category   If you've assigned categories to your journal entries and other items, you can display your journal entries by category in the timeline view.

Entry List   Displays entries in a table with columns labeled Entry Type, Subject, Start, Duration, Contact, and Categories.

Last Seven Days   Displays entries in an entry list, but includes only those entries dated within the last seven days.

Phone Calls   Lists all entries that are phone calls.

Sort Journal Entries   You can click the heading bar—Subject, Start, or Duration—in any Entry list view to sort the items in that column in ascending or descending order.

In this lesson, you learned to manually and automatically create journal entries and to change views in the Journal. In the next lesson, you'll learn to create notes.

CREATING NOTES

In this lesson, you learn to create, sort, and view notes.

CREATING NOTES

If you've ever used a paper sticky note to remind yourself of tasks, ideas, or other brief annotations, Outlook's Notes are for you. Notes are very similar to paper sticky notes. You can use Notes to write down reminders, names, phone numbers, directions, or anything else you need to remember. In Outlook, all notes are kept in the Notes folder. You'll have to remember to look at the folder so you can view your notes.

To create a note, follow these steps:

1. In the Notes folder, choose Note, New Note or click the New Note button on the Standard toolbar. A note appears, ready for you to type your text (see Figure 17.1).

2. Enter the text for your note.

 The Long and Short of It Notes don't have to be brief. **TIP** You can enter pages and pages of text if you want. As you type, the page scrolls for you; use the arrow keys and the Page Up/Page Down keys to move through the note text.

3. When you finish, click the Close (X) button to close the note. You can reopen a note and enter as much text or edit text as you need to.

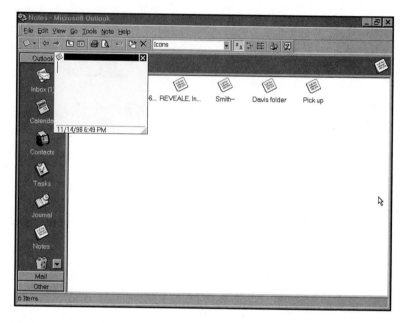

FIGURE 17.1 A note automatically includes the date and time it was created.

If you press Enter after entering text in the note, you create both a line break and a title of sorts at the same time. Only the text before the hard return is displayed when the note is closed. If you do not add a hard return, but instead enter the note text so it automatically wraps from line to line, the entire note text appears below the note in Icons view.

SETTING NOTE OPTIONS

You can change the default color and size of your notes. You also can change the default font used for your notes. To set note options, follow these steps:

1. In the Notes folder, choose Tools, Options. The Options dialog box appears with the Tasks/Notes tab displayed (see Figure 17.2.)

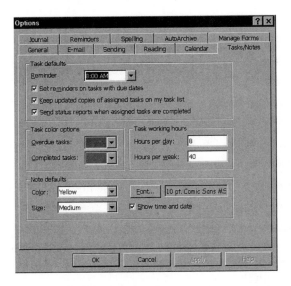

FIGURE 17.2 Customize your notes.

2. In the Note Defaults area of the dialog box, click the Color drop-down arrow and select a new default color for your notes. You can change the color to yellow, blue, green, pink, or white. The default is yellow.

3. Open the Size drop-down list and choose Small, Medium, or Large for the size of the notes. The default is Medium.

4. If you would prefer not to show the time and date on your notes, deselect the Show Time and Date check box.

5. To change the font, click the Font button. The Font dialog box appears. Change the font, font style, size, color, and other options, and then click OK.

MANAGING INDIVIDUAL NOTES

To open a note, double-click it in the Notes folder. You can edit the text in an open note as you would edit any text. To move a note, drag its title bar. You also can delete, forward, or print notes; you can change the color of individual notes; and you can specify categories for your notes.

Click an open note's Control-menu button to display a menu with the following commands:

New Note   Creates a new note but leaves the first note open.

Save As   Enables you to save the note and its contents.

Delete   Deletes a note and its contents. (You also can delete a note by selecting it in the Notes list and pressing the Delete key.)

Forward   Enables you to send the note as an attachment in an e-mail message.

Cut, Copy, Paste   Enables you to select text from the note and cut or copy it to the Clipboard. The Paste command enables you to paste items on the Clipboard at the insertion point in the note.

Color   Choose another color for the individual note.

Categories   Enter or choose a category.

Print   Print the contents of the note.

Close   Closes the note. (You also can click the Close (X) button in the note's title bar.) A closed note appears in the Notes folder.

VIEWING NOTES

The Notes folder provides various views for organizing and viewing your notes. You can also sort notes in any entry list view by right-clicking the heading bar—Subject, Created, Categories, and so on—and selecting the sort method.

The default view is Icons, but you can change the view using the Current View drop-down list in the Standard toolbar. Figure 17.3 shows the Notes folder in the default view.

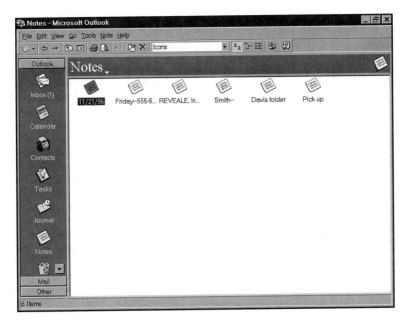

FIGURE 17.3   This view displays the notes in Icons view.

You can choose to display your Notes folder in any of the following views:

Icons   Displays the notes as note icons with the message (or a portion of the message) displayed below the icon.

Notes List   Displays the notes in a list, showing the title and note contents in the Subject column, the creation date and time, and the categories.

Last Seven Days   Displays all notes written in the last seven days, by subject, creation date, and categories.

By Category   Displays the categories; double-click a category to show its contents.

By Color   Displays notes by their color. Double-click a color to display the notes.

In this lesson, you learned to create, sort, and view notes. In the next lesson, you will learn to print in Outlook.

PRINTING IN OUTLOOK

In this lesson, you learn to print items in Outlook, change the page setup, preview an item before printing it, and change printer properties.

CHOOSING PAGE SETUP

In Outlook, before you print you choose the print style you will use. Each folder—Inbox, Calendar, Contacts, and so on—offers various print styles, and each style displays the data on the page in a different way.

Page In Outlook, this is the area of the paper that will actually be printed on. You might, for example, print two or four pages on a single sheet of paper.

Print Style The combination of paper and page settings that control printed output.

You can choose from Outlook's built-in print styles, modify the default print styles, or create your own print styles. These lists show the default print styles available for each folder.

The Inbox, Contacts, and Tasks use the following two styles; the Journal and Notes use only the Memo Style.

 Table Style Displays data in columns and rows on an 8.5-by-11 sheet, portrait orientation, .5-inch margins.

 Memo Style Displays data with a header of information about the message and then straight text on an 8.5-by-11 sheet, portrait orientation, .5-inch margins.

The Calendar folder provides the Memo style, plus the following styles:

 Daily Style   Displays one day's appointments on one page on an 8.5-by-11 sheet, portrait orientation, .5-inch margins.

 Weekly Style   Displays one week's appointments per page on an 8.5-by-11 sheet, portrait orientation, .5-inch margins.

 Monthly Style   Displays one month's appointments per page on an 8.5-by-11 sheet, landscape orientation, .5-inch margins.

 Tri-fold Style   Displays the daily calendar, task list, and weekly calendar on an 8.5-by-11 sheet, landscape orientation, .5-inch margins.

The Contacts folder provides the Memo style, plus the following styles:

 Card Style   Two columns and headings on an 8.5-by-11 sheet, portrait orientation, .5-inch margins.

 Small Booklet Style   One-column page that equals 1/8 of a sheet of paper—so that eight pages are on one 8.5-by-11 sheet of paper with .5-inch margins. Then the portrait orientation applies to the 1/8 pages.

 Medium Booklet Style   One column that equals 1/4 of a sheet of paper—so that four pages are on one 8.5-by-11 sheet of paper. Portrait orientation with .5-inch margins.

 Phone Directory Style   One column, 8.5-by-11 sheet of paper, portrait orientation with .5-inch margins.

 Page Setup Only Matters in Printing   No matter how you set up your pages, it will not affect your view of tasks, calendars, or other Outlook items on-screen. Page setup only applies to a printed job.

You can view, modify, and create new page setups in Outlook. To view or edit a page setup, follow these steps:

1. Change to the folder for which you're setting the page.

2. Choose File, Page Setup. A secondary menu appears that lists the available print types.

3. Select the print type you want to view or edit, and the Page Setup dialog box appears (see Figure 18.1).

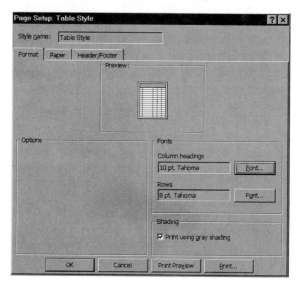

FIGURE 18.1   Customize the print type to suit yourself.

4. Click the Format tab to view and/or edit the page type, to choose options (in some cases), and to change fonts.

5. Click the Paper tab to view and/or edit paper size, page size, margins, and orientation.

6. Click the Header/Footer tab to view and/or edit headers for your pages.

PREVIEWING BEFORE PRINTING

You can choose to preview an item before printing it so you're sure it looks the way you want it to look. If you do not like the way an item looks in preview, you can change the page setup.

Before you display an item in print preview, you must change to the folder containing the item you want to print. Then you can choose to preview the item in any of the following ways:

- Click the Print Preview button in the Page Setup dialog box.

- Choose File, Print Preview.

- Click the Print Preview button on the Standard toolbar.

- Click the Preview button in the Print dialog box.

Figure 18.2 shows a calendar and task list in Print Preview.

Mouse pointer changes to a magnifying glass.

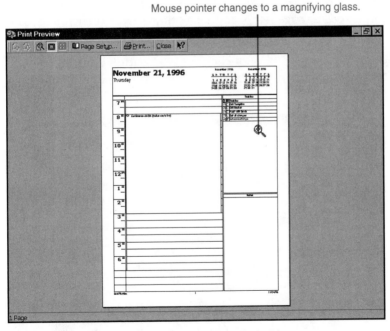

FIGURE 18.2   Preview the item before printing it.

You can change the page setup by clicking the Page Setup button; the Page Setup dialog box appears. Click the Print button to send the job to the printer. Click the Close button to exit Print Preview and return to the Outlook folder.

Enlarge the View When the mouse pointer looks like a magnifying glass with a plus sign in it, you can click to enlarge the page. When the mouse pointer looks like a magnifying glass with a minus sign in it, you can click to reduce the view again.

PRINTING ITEMS

After you choose the print style and preview an item to make sure it's what you want, you can print the item. You can indicate the number of copies you want to print, select a printer, change the print style or page setup, and set a print range. When you're ready to print an item, follow these steps:

 1. Choose File, Print or click the Print button on the Standard toolbar. The Print dialog box appears, as shown in Figure 18.3.

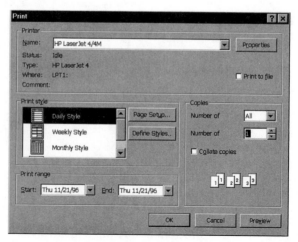

FIGURE 18.3 Set the printing options before printing the item.

2. In the Printer area of the dialog box, choose a different printer from the Name drop-down list if necessary.

In a Hurry? If your computer is on a network and you notice the Status of the selected printer is Busy or Paused, for example, choose a different printer from the drop-down list.

3. In the Print Style area, choose a print style from the list. You also can edit the page setup (with the Page Setup button) or edit or create a new style (with the Define Styles button).

4. In the Copies area of the dialog box, choose All, Even, or Odd in Number of Pages and enter the number of copies you want to print. Click the Collate Copies check box if you want Outlook to automatically assemble multiple copies.

5. Set the print range with the options in that area. (The Print Range options vary depending on the type of item you're printing.)

6. Click OK to print the item.

SETTING PRINTER PROPERTIES

Whether you're printing to a printer connected directly to your computer or to a printer on the network, you can set printer properties. The properties you set apply to all print jobs you send to the printer until you change the properties again.

Printer Properties Configurations specific to a printer connected to your computer or to the network. Printer properties include paper orientation, paper source, graphics settings, fonts, and print quality.

Access Denied?   If you cannot change the printer properties to a network printer, it's probably because the network administrator has set the printer's configuration and
you're not allowed access to the settings. If you need to
change printer properties and cannot access the printer's
Properties dialog box, talk to your network administrator.

To set printer properties, open the Print dialog box (by choosing
File, Print). In the Printer area, select a printer from the Name
drop-down list, and then click the Properties button. The printers'
Properties dialog boxes differ depending on the make and model
of printer.

Most likely, you'll be able to set paper size, page orientation, and
paper source using options on a Paper tab in the dialog box. In
addition, you might see a Graphics tab, in which you can set the
resolution, intensity, and graphics mode of your printer. A Fonts
tab enables you to set options on TrueType fonts, font cartridges,
and so on. You might also find a Device Options tab, in which
you can set print quality and other options. For more information
about your printer, read the documentation that came with it.

In this lesson, you learned to print items in Outlook, change the
page setup, preview an item before printing it, and change printer
properties. In the next lesson, you will learn to manage your files
and Outlook items.

SAVING, OPENING, AND FINDING OUTLOOK ITEMS

In this lesson, you learn to save items, open items, and find items in Outlook.

SAVING ITEMS

Generally, when you finish adding a new task, appointment, meeting, contact, or other item, Outlook automatically saves that item for you or you're prompted to save the item yourself. You also can save most items in Outlook for use in other applications by using the Save As command. After you save an item by naming it, you can open that same item and edit, print, or otherwise use the saved file in Windows applications that support the file type. You might save an item—a journal entry or appointment page, for example—so you can refer to it later, edit the original, or keep it as a record.

Save As When you save an item using the File, Save As command, you can designate a drive, directory, and new file name for that item, as well as a file type.

File Type A file type is the same thing as a file format. When you save a file, you specify a file type that identifies the file as one that can be opened in specific applications. For example, the file extension .DOC identifies a file type that you can open in Word, and the extension .TXT represents a text-only format you can open in nearly any word processor or other application.

To save an item, follow these steps:

1. In the folder containing the item you want to save, choose File, Save As. The Save As dialog box appears (see Figure 19.1).

Figure 19.1   Save items as files for use in other programs, as copies of the originals, or for later use.

 Why Is Save As Dimmed?   When the Save As command is dimmed, you must first select an item—an appointment, meeting, task, note, or whatever—before you can save it.

2. From the Save In drop-down list, choose the drive to which you want to save the file. From the folders on that drive, select the one you want to save to.

3. In the Save As Type drop-down list, choose a file type. You can save the file in the following file types:

    Text Only   Saves in an ASCII format that you can use in other applications, such as Word, Notepad, and so on.

    RTF Text Format   Saves in rich text format. You also can use this format in Word, Outlook, or Lotus Notes, for example.

Outlook Template   Saves as a template (or style sheet) that you can use as a basis for other items.

Message Format   Saves in a format you can use in your e-mail messages.

4. Enter a name for the item in the File Name text box, or accept the default.

5. Click the Save button.

OPENING AND USING SAVED ITEMS

After you save items, you can open and use them in Outlook and other applications. If, for example, you saved a contact as a message file, you can insert that file into a message and send the contact's name, address, and other information to someone through an e-mail message. You can save other items, such as meeting information from your calendar, as a text file you can open in Notepad or Word to edit, format, print, or otherwise modify the file.

OPENING AND USING AN RTF FILE

You can open RTF files in many word processing programs—Word, Notepad, WordPad, and so on. To open an RTF file in another Windows application, choose File, Open. In the Open dialog box, choose Rich Text Format (or RTF Text Format) in the Files of Type drop-down list. The saved files appear in the file list. Select the file and click the Open button.

 RTF Isn't Listed?   If RTF isn't listed in the application's Files of Type list box, see if Text Only is listed. You can also save Outlook items as Text Only.

Figure 19.2 shows an e-mail message saved as an RTF file and opened in Word. After opening a file, you can format it, cut or copy items to it, insert objects, print, edit, and otherwise manipulate the file. In addition, the attachment to the message can be opened and read within the saved RTF files.

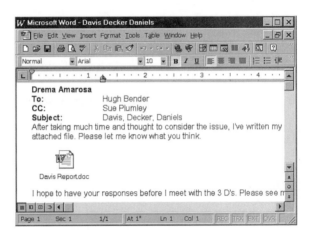

FIGURE 19.2 Exchanging data between applications makes your work quicker and easier.

OPENING AND USING A TEXT-ONLY FILE

You open a text-only file in much the same way you open an RTF file. In Notepad, for example, choose File, Open and choose Text Documents as the file type in the Open dialog box. Files saved as text-only do not retain any formatting; however, you can select the text and format it in the destination application.

USING A MESSAGE TEXT FILE

After you save an item as a message text file, you can insert the item into an e-mail message to send. Suppose you saved a contact's information or an especially long note that you want to share with someone else; you can insert the file as an object into a message and send the e-mail as you normally would. Then the recipient can open the message and the message file.

Files As Objects As described in Lesson 10, you can insert any existing file as an object into any Windows document that supports OLE.

To insert a message file into a message, open the message and choose Insert, Object. In the Insert Object dialog box, choose Create from File. Enter the path and file name and click OK. Figure 19.3 shows a message file in the text of an e-mail.

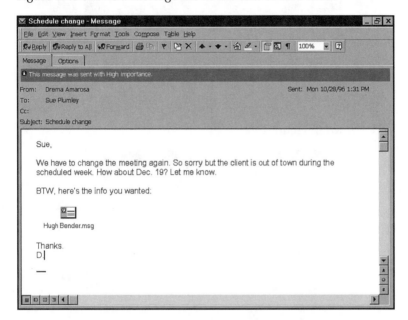

FIGURE 19.3   Open the MSG file by double-clicking its icon.

FINDING ITEMS

Outlook provides a method you can use to locate items on your computer. You can search for messages, files, journal entries, notes, tasks, contacts, or appointments. You can search for specific words, categories, priority, and other criteria that you stipulate. Outlook's Find feature can be especially useful if your folders become full, and locating items on your own is difficult.

Criteria Guidelines you set in the Find dialog box that Outlook uses to find items, such as messages, contacts, or appointments. Included in the criteria you set may be the date an item was created, the title or subject of the item, or specific text within the item.

To find an item in Outlook, follow these steps:

 1. Choose Tools, Find Items or click the Find Items button on the Standard toolbar. The Find dialog box appears, as shown in Figure 19.4.

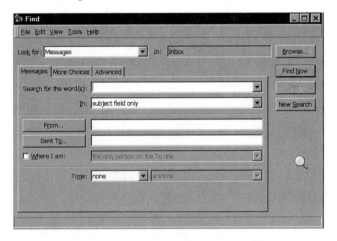

Figure 19.4 You can search for messages, appointments, and other items.

 My Dialog Box Is Different The Find dialog box in Figure 19.4 was opened from the Inbox. If you open the Find dialog box from Calendar, Tasks, or any other folder, the options in the dialog box relate to the item for which you're searching.

2. In any Find dialog box, choose the item for which you want to search in the Look For drop-down list.

3. Click the Browse button to display the Select Folder(s) dialog box, from which you can choose the folder to search.

4. On the first tab, which is named for the item you select in the Look For list, you can enter specific words to search for, fields you want to search, dates, contact names, file types, and so on. The second tab, More Choices, offers additional options to add to the search, such as item size and category. Set the options you want on both tabs.

Narrow the Search The more options you select and specify in the Find dialog box, the more you narrow the search; fewer items will match the search criteria. However, when you select more options, the search could take longer.

5. When you're ready to find the item(s), click the Find Now button. The Find dialog box extends to display a list of items Outlook finds that match the search criteria. In addition to the name of the item, the search results also show the folder in which you'll find the item, along with other item details.

You can perform a new search by clicking the New Search button, which clears the text boxes and previously selected options, and entering new criteria. If you want to pause or stop a search that's taking too long, click the Stop button.

Fast Find When you're in the Inbox, an extra Find command appears on the Tools menu: Find All. With the Find All command, you can choose to find all messages related to the selected message or all messages from the sender of the selected message. The Find dialog box appears, displaying a list of the matching messages.

USING THE ADVANCED SEARCH

The Find dialog box includes an Advanced tab that contains options you can use to perform more detailed searches than you can with the other options in the dialog box. On the Advanced tab, you can set multiple search criteria such as a category, author, and subject or a message flag and priority setting. To use the Advanced tab in the Find dialog box, follow these steps:

1. Open the Find dialog box by choosing Tools, Find Items.

2. (Optional) Set any criteria you want on the Item tab and More Choices tab.

3. Click the Advanced tab.

4. On the Advanced tab, choose the Field drop-down list to define more criteria. You can choose from multiple commands, each of which displays a secondary menu. The commands and secondary menus depend on the item for which you're searching. The following are a few of the fields for the Message item:

   Frequently-Used Fields   Includes fields such as Categories, Created, Duration, Location, Recurrence, and Subject.

   Date/Time Fields   Includes Created, Duration, Start, and so on.

   All Appointment Fields   Includes such fields as Importance, Meeting Status, Notes, Recurring, Reminder, and Resources.

   All Mail Fields   Includes Categories, Created, Expires, Subject, and so on.

   All Tasks Fields   Includes % Complete, Conversation, Due Date, Mileage, Notes, Owner, Priority, and so on.

   All Journal Fields   Includes Billing Information, Company, Entry Type, Sensitivity, Start, and so on.

5. After you choose a field, select the condition from the Condition drop-down list. Conditions include such

constraints as whether the field is empty, and exactly what values or word the field contains. (For example, you might choose the field **Category** and the condition **Contains**.)

6. If you choose a condition that specifies the contents of the field, next you fill in the Value. A value might be a name, word, note color, or priority found in the item.

7. Click the Add to List button. Any criteria you set is listed in the Find Items That Match These Criteria list box; items are added as you select them in the Advanced tab.

8. When you've finished setting criteria, click Find Now.

Figure 19.5 shows the Advanced tab before adding the final criterion for which to search. The results of this search will show any messages that contain the words "Time Applied" in the Billing Information field, and do not contain the words "Bender Printing" in the Message text.

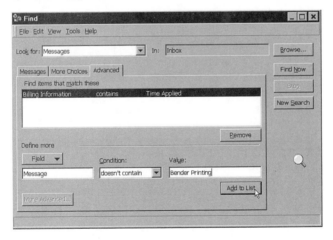

FIGURE 19.5   Set advanced criteria to find specific items.

In this lesson, you learned to save items, open items, and find items in Outlook. In the next lesson, you will learn to integrate items between Outlook folders.

20 LESSON
INTEGRATING ITEMS

In this lesson, you learn to use various items in Outlook together (to create a task or an appointment from a mail message or to create a document within Outlook, for example).

CREATING A TASK FROM A MAIL MESSAGE

You can use a mail message to create a task quickly and easily in Outlook. Instead of printing the message and then opening your Task List to add the information, you can create the task by using drag-and-drop copying. For more information about using the Tasks folder, see Lesson 15, "Creating a Task List."

You Don't Lose the Message When you use a message to create another item, Outlook copies the message so that the original message remains in the Inbox.

To create a task from a mail message, follow these steps:

1. Open the Inbox folder.

2. Click and drag the unopened mail message from the Inbox window to the Tasks icon on the Outlook Bar. The Task dialog box opens (see Figure 20.1).

3. Change the subject or other data if you want, and then set any options for the task (such as due date, priority, reminders, categories, and so on).

4. Click the Save and Close button, and Outlook adds the task to your list.

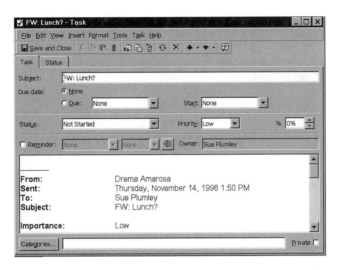

FIGURE 20.1 Create a task from an e-mail message.

CREATING AN APPOINTMENT FROM A MAIL MESSAGE

In addition to creating tasks from messages, you can create an appointment from a mail message. When you create the appointment, you can set a time and date for the appointment, invite attendees to the appointment, create a meeting, and otherwise set options for the appointment. For more information about creating appointments, see Lesson 12, "Using the Calendar."

To create an appointment from a message, follow these steps:

1. Open the Inbox and locate the message you want to use.

2. Drag the unopened message from the Inbox window to the Calendar folder on the Outlook Bar. The Appointment dialog box opens with some information automatically filled in (see Figure 20.2).

3. Add the location to the appointment and make any desired changes in the Subject, Start Time, or End Time boxes, or in any other of the options.

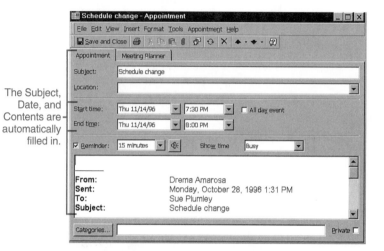

The Subject, Date, and Contents are automatically filled in.

FIGURE 20.2   Create an appointment using the data in a mail message.

4. Click the Save and Close button to complete the appointment.

CREATE A NOTE FROM ANY ITEM

Just as you can create tasks and appointments from a mail message, you also can create a note from any item in Outlook. Suppose someone e-mailed you information about a product or service that you want to add to a report; you can simply create a note with the information on it. Or suppose you want to call someone at a certain time later in the day. You can create a note from your contact entry so you won't forget.

You can create a note from a mail message, appointment or meeting, contact, task, or journal entry. After you create the note, you can edit the text in the note without affecting the original item.

To create a note from any Outlook item, drag the item into the Notes folder in the Outlook Bar. Outlook creates and displays the note, and you can edit the text if you want. For more information about notes, see Lesson 17, "Creating Notes."

USING OUTLOOK TEMPLATES

Outlook includes many templates on which you can base new messages, appointments, tasks, and so on. You use a template when you want to create a new item. The e-mail templates, for example, supply an Untitled Message window with decorative fonts and graphics you can use to add pizzazz to your message.

To use an Outlook template, follow these steps:

1. Choose File, New.

2. In the secondary menu that appears, select Choose Template. The Choose Template dialog box appears with several templates from which to choose (see Figure 20.3).

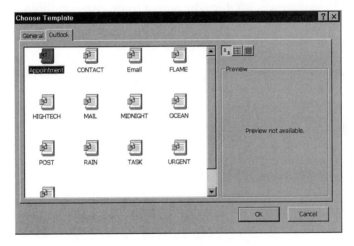

FIGURE 20.3   Base your new item on a specific template.

3. Select the template you want to use and click OK. Outlook displays the message, task, appointment, or other window in which you can create your item.

In this lesson, you learned to use various items in Outlook together—to create a task and an appointment from a mail message and to create a document within Outlook. In the next lesson, you will learn to share data with other Office applications.

LESSON 21

SHARING DATA WITH OFFICE APPLICATIONS

In this lesson, you learn to share data between Outlook and other Office applications.

CREATING A NEW OFFICE DOCUMENT

You can create a new Office document from within Outlook; for example, you can write a letter, write a report, create a spreadsheet, and so on. To create the document, you work in the actual Office application, such as Word, using that application's tools and features. When you save the document, a shortcut saves to Outlook so you can quickly and easily open the document at any time.

To create a new Office document, follow these steps:

1. Choose File, New, Office Document. The New Office Document dialog box appears, as shown in Figure 21.1.

 I Don't See the New Document Dialog Box In order for this dialog box to appear, Office must be installed and you must have at least one Office template located in the Microsoft Office Templates folder.

2. Select the template for an Excel worksheet or chart, a Word document, or a PowerPoint presentation and click OK. Select one of the options, and the template opens in a document window. Enter and format the text. Then use the menus to check spelling, create pictures, and otherwise manage the document as you would in a word processor.

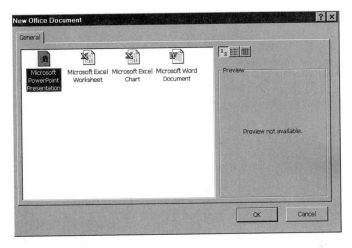

FIGURE 21.1 Select the document template on which to base your new document.

3. To print the document, choose File, Print.

4. To save the document, choose File, Save As. The Save As dialog box appears.

5. Enter a file name and file type, and choose a location.

6. Choose File, Close to close the document and the document window. The document is added to the Outlook item you were in when you created it.

To open the document for editing, printing, or other manipulation, double-click it.

CREATING AN OUTLOOK ITEM FROM AN OFFICE FILE

You can create an appointment from a Word document, a mail message from an Excel document, or one of many other items by dragging a file to an Outlook item. This capability is great for when you want to include data in a mail message or record items in your journal. Sharing data between Office applications makes your work easier and more efficient.

To create an Outlook item from an Office file, follow these steps:

1. Open the Explorer window and the Outlook window so you can see both on-screen at the same time (see Figure 21.2).

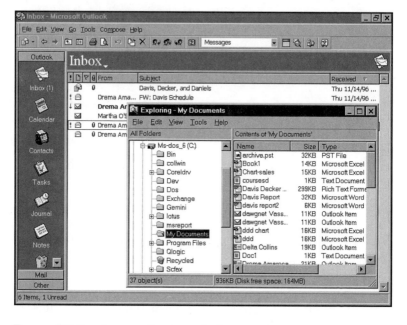

FIGURE 21.2   Arrange the two windows on-screen so you can drag from one to the other.

2. In the Explorer window, select the file from which you want to create an Outlook item, and then drag it to the folder in the Outlook Bar. For example, drag a worksheet to the Inbox to create a message.

3. The new item dialog box opens, with the Office file represented as an icon in the item. Enter any details, such as subject, dates, and so on, and then save the item as usual.

Shortcut   Drag an Outlook item onto the Windows desktop to create a copy of the item that you can open quickly.

IMPORTING AND EXPORTING FILES

You can import files to Outlook and export files from Outlook to other Office applications. When you import, you're opening another Office application's file in a format that Outlook can read so you can use the file's contents in Outlook. When you export, you're saving Outlook data in a format that one of the other Office applications can use.

IMPORTING

You might import files from Access, FoxPro, dBase, Schedule+, Excel, or some other application for use in Outlook.

To import data, follow these steps:

1. In Outlook, choose File, Import and Export. The Import and Export Wizard appears (see Figure 21.3).

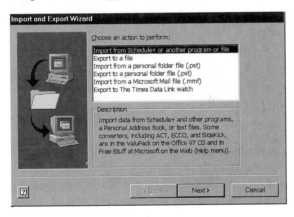

FIGURE 21.3   Import files to use in Outlook.

   Wizard In Microsoft Office products, a wizard is a series of dialog boxes containing instructions and options. A wizard helps you complete a task.

2. Choose Import from Schedule+ or Another Program or File and click the Next button. The second wizard dialog box appears.

3. Scroll through the list using the vertical scroll bar if necessary, and choose the type of file you want to import from the list. Click the Next button.

Word's Not There!   You won't see Microsoft Word on the list, but you can still import a Word file. Select the Comma Separated Values (Windows) option to import a Word file that you've converted to text-only; first you'll have to use Word to save the Word file in Text Only format.

4. In the third wizard dialog box, enter the path and the file name in the File to Import text box, or click the Browse button and select the file from the Browse dialog box. Set any options in the Options area of the dialog box and click the Next button.

5. In the fourth wizard dialog box, select the folder in which you want to import the file and click Next.

Exporting

You can export Outlook files to Access, Excel, Word, and so on for use with other applications. For example, you might export an e-mail message to Word as a memo, or you might export data from your journal into an Excel worksheet. When you export a file, you're saving the file's contents in a format another application can open and use.

To export a file, follow these steps:

1. Select the item you want to export as a file and choose File, Import and Export. The Import and Export Wizard dialog box appears.

2. Choose Export to a File and click Next.

3. In the second wizard dialog box, select the folder to export from and click Next.

4. In the third wizard dialog box, select the file type and click Next.

5. In the fourth wizard dialog box, enter the path and name of the file to be exported, and then click Next.

6. Select a destination folder and click Next.

LINKING AND EMBEDDING OBJECTS

You can use Windows OLE to share data between Office applications. Object Linking and Embedding is a feature that most Windows applications support. OLE enables you to share data between a source application and a destination application, ensuring that all documents are updated automatically and in a timely fashion. For example, you can link an Excel worksheet to a mail message to ensure that the data you send with the message is up-to-date and accurate. You also can embed objects into mail messages in Outlook.

One of the biggest advantages of using OLE is that you can edit an object by double-clicking it. When you do, the file is updated in both the source and the destination applications with the changes you've made. You can use existing files or create new files for both linking and embedding.

Linking Creating a bridge between two applications so that the data in one application is copied exactly into the second application and updated automatically whenever changes are made.

Embedding Using one application to create an object within another application.

Source The application or document in which the object was created.

Destination The application or document into which the object is copied or embedded.

Object The Word document, Excel worksheet, Outlook note, or other item that is linked or embedded.

LINKING OBJECTS

Outlook enables you to link data between two or more applications when you want to ensure that all data is kept up-to-date automatically. If, for example, you link an Excel worksheet to an Outlook message, each time you make a change to the numbers in the worksheet, those numbers also change in the linked data in the message.

To link an object between Outlook and another application, follow these steps:

1. In Outlook, create a new mail message or reply, and then place the insertion point in the body of the message.

2. Choose Insert, Object. The Object dialog box appears.

3. Choose the Create from File tab. The Object dialog box changes to look like the one shown in Figure 21.4.

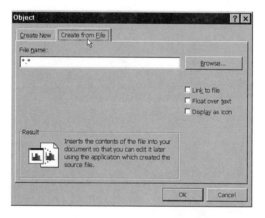

FIGURE 21.4 Create a link to an existing object.

4. Enter the path and file name of the object you want to link in the File Name text box, or click the Browse button and select the file.

5. Select the Link check box and click OK. Outlook inserts a copy of the object in the message text. The link remains—guaranteeing updated information—until you send the message.

EMBEDDING OBJECTS

You might want to embed a new or existing file, such as a Word table and text, into an e-mail message to send to someone in your company. When you embed the data, the recipient has only to double-click the embedded object to open, read, edit, and/or print the file's contents. Note, however, that embedded data (unlike linked data) isn't updated when a source file changes.

To embed an object in Outlook, follow these steps:

1. In Outlook, create a new mail message or reply, and then place the insertion point in the body of the message.

2. Choose Insert, Object. The Insert Object dialog box appears.

3. Choose Create New, and a list of available Object Types appears in the dialog box.

4. Select the object type you want and click OK. Windows inserts a window into the message, from which you can create a document, spreadsheet, chart, or other object.

For example, if you choose to insert a spreadsheet, Windows creates a window within the message that looks like an Excel worksheet. In addition, the Outlook message window changes to look similar to Excel's, as shown in Figure 21.5.

When you finish entering data, click outside of the frame to return to Outlook. At any time, you can double-click anywhere in the frame to edit the data.

Why the Entire Excel Workbook?   If you create an object from an existing Excel workbook, Outlook inserts the whole workbook into the item. You can only display one worksheet at a time, however. Double-click the Excel object to choose a different worksheet.

Excel commands on the menus   Excel buttons

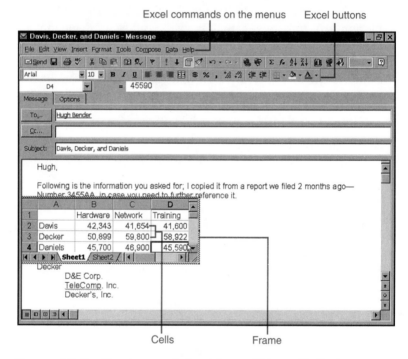

Cells   Frame

FIGURE 21.5   Create a worksheet from within an Outlook message.

In this lesson, you learned to share data between Outlook and other Office applications. In the next lesson, you'll learn to archive items.

ARCHIVING ITEMS

22

In this lesson, you learn to use AutoArchive and to archive files, retrieve archived files, and delete archived files.

USING AUTOARCHIVE

You can set an option in Outlook to automatically archive your mail messages into files periodically. The AutoArchive feature cleans your Inbox for you without deleting any messages.

 Archive To save items to a file that can be opened at any time and printed, viewed, or otherwise used. You might, for example, want to archive some of your mail messages to keep for your records instead of leaving those messages in your Inbox. Archived items are removed from the folder and copied to an archive file.

To use AutoArchive, follow these steps:

1. Choose Tools, Options. The Options dialog box appears.

2. Click the AutoArchive tab.

3. Click the AutoArchive Every *xx* check box to display the rest of the items in the dialog box (see Figure 22.1).

4. Choose from the following options:

    AutoArchive Every *x* Days at Startup   Enter a number for how often (in days) you want Outlook to automatically archive items. If you enter **14**, for example, when you start Outlook on the 14th day, it automatically archives the contents of your folders into an archive file.

Prompt Before AutoArchive If you check this, Outlook displays a dialog box each time it is about to perform the AutoArchive; you can click OK or Cancel to continue or stop the operation.

Delete Expired Items When AutoArchiving (E-Mail Folders Only) Check this box to have Outlook delete messages from the Inbox after archiving them.

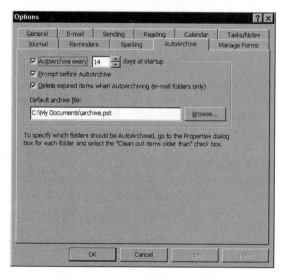

FIGURE 22.1 Specify options for automatically archiving items into files.

5. In the Default Archive File text box, enter a path to where you want to save the file, and name it (if you don't want to use the default).

6. Click OK to close the dialog box.

In addition to setting the AutoArchive options in the Options dialog box, each folder—Inbox, Tasks, Calendar, and so on—has additional AutoArchive options you can set.

To set individual folder's AutoArchive options, follow these steps:

1. Right-click the folder in the Outlook Bar to display the shortcut menu.

2. Choose Properties. The item's Properties dialog box appears.

3. Choose the AutoArchive tab. Figure 22.2 shows the Inbox's AutoArchive tab.

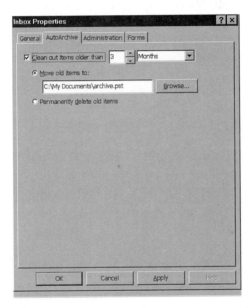

FIGURE 22.2   Set AutoArchive options for individual folders.

4. Set the options you want in the dialog box. You can change the length of time you want the archived files to be saved before they're deleted or saved to another file, and you can enter a path and file name for the second save.

5. Click OK to close the dialog box.

ARCHIVING MANUALLY

You can choose to archive one or two folders or all folders manually whenever you're ready to create an archive file. If you choose to do it yourself, you control exactly how and when archives are created.

To create an archive, follow these steps:

1. Choose File, Archive. The Archive dialog box appears (see Figure 22.3).

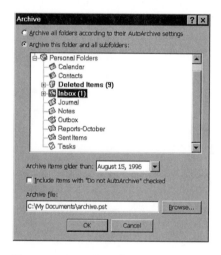

FIGURE 22.3   Enter settings for manual archiving.

2. Choose one of the following options:

    Archive All Folders According to Their AutoArchive Settings   Use this option to save archives of each folder using the settings you select in the AutoArchive tab of the folder's Properties dialog box.

    Archive This Folder and All Subfolders   Select this option to archive the selected folder.

3. Enter a date in the Archive Items Older Than text box, or select a date from the drop-down calendar.

4. In the Archive File text box, enter a path and file name with which to save the file.

5. Click OK to archive the selected folder(s).

RETRIEVING ARCHIVED FILES

You can retrieve an archived file by importing it to the original file. When you retrieve an archived file, it becomes a part of your Outlook folder just as it was before you archived it.

Follow these steps to retrieve an archived file:

1. Choose File, Import and Export. The Import and Export Wizard dialog box appears.

2. Choose Import from a Personal Folders File (*PST) and click the Next button.

3. In the second wizard dialog box, enter the path and the file name of the archived file.

4. Select any one of the following options, and then click the Next button:

   Replace Duplicates with Items Imported to overwrite any copies of the data with imported items.

   Allow Duplicates to Be Created to create duplicates of the items instead of overwriting them.

   Do Not Import Duplicates to preserve the originals in the folder instead of overwriting them with items from the archived file.

5. In the third wizard dialog box, choose the folder into which you want to import. (The default is to import the archived item to the Personal Folders area; you may have created subfolders into which you want to import.)

6. Click the Finish button, and Outlook imports the archived files.

DELETING ARCHIVED FILES

The easiest way to delete archived files is by using the Windows Explorer. However, you can also delete files from the Find Files and Folders dialog box or from My Computer (both Windows applications).

To delete an archived file, follow these steps:

1. Open the Explorer and locate the files. Archived files are saved with a .PST extension in the My Documents folder (by default) or any other folder you designate.

2. Open the folder containing the files and select the file(s) you want to delete.

3. Press the Delete key, or drag the file(s) to the Recycle Bin.

4. Empty the Recycle Bin by right-clicking the Bin icon and choosing Empty Recycle Bin.

5. Close the Explorer by clicking the Close (X) button.

In this lesson, you learned to use AutoArchive and to archive files, retrieve archived files, and delete archived files. In the next lesson, you will learn to customize Outlook.

CUSTOMIZING OUTLOOK

In this lesson, you will learn to set e-mail, calendar, and other options in Outlook.

SETTING GENERAL OPTIONS

General options include choices that can make your work more comfortable or efficient. For example, you can choose to view large toolbar buttons if you have trouble with seeing or clicking the small icons, or you can choose to empty the Deleted Items folder automatically when you exit Outlook.

To customize general options, follow these steps:

1. Choose Tools, Options. The Options dialog box appears.

2. Click the General tab.

3. In the General Settings area, check the boxes of the options you want to activate, which are listed here:

   Warn Before Permanently Deleting Items

   Empty the Deleted Items Folder Upon Exiting

   When Selecting Text, Automatically Select Entire Word

   When Online, Synchronize all Folders Upon Exiting

   Provide Feedback with Sound

   Large Toolbar Icons

4. In the Startup Settings area, choose Prompt for a Profile to Be Used or Always Use This Profile.

Profile   A group of settings that control how your mail is delivered, received, and stored in Outlook, and the software used to transfer your mail, such as Microsoft Mail, Microsoft Exchange, or Lotus Notes.

5. When you finish setting the options on this tab, do one of the following things:

    Click Apply to set these options, and then click another tab to customize the options on it.

    Click OK to accept the changes and close the Options dialog box.

    Click Cancel to void any changes you made and close the dialog box.

SETTING E-MAIL OPTIONS

Use the E-mail tab to set options that govern how the program deals with new mail and how new mail is processed. Figure 23.1 shows the Options dialog box with the E-mail tab displayed.

To set e-mail options, follow these steps:

1. Choose Tools, Options. The Options dialog box appears.

2. Click the E-mail tab.

3. In the Check for New Mail On list box, check all types of e-mail you want to receive.

Check for New Mail?   The mail types listed in the Check for New Mail On list box are added when you add a new profile to Outlook. You add a profile by choosing Tools, Services.

4. In the When New Items Arrive area, choose the options you want to apply to your setup.

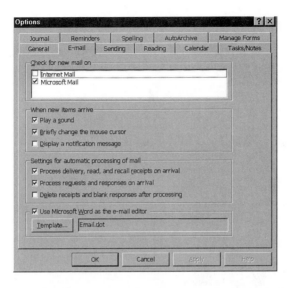

FIGURE 23.1 Customize e-mail options to suit your needs.

5. In the Settings for Automatic Processing of Mail area,
   check the boxes next to the options you want to apply
   (described here):   ·

   Process Delivery, Read, and Recall, Receipts on Arrival
   When this is checked, Outlook automatically records
   status when an item is delivered, read, or recalled.

   Process Requests and Responses on Arrival   When this is
   checked, Outlook automatically places meeting requests
   on your Calendar and responses to meeting requests in
   your Meeting Planner.

   Delete Receipts and Blank Responses After Processing
   When this is checked, Outlook automatically deletes
   responses to meeting requests that have no comments
   when mail is delivered, read, or recalled.

6. When you're done, click Apply to save the changes and
   view another tab, or click OK to save the changes and
   close the dialog box.

SETTING SENDING OPTIONS

Sending options allow you to control the font used for new messages, tracking options, and choices for dealing with sent items.

Follow these steps to set sending options:

1. Choose Tools, Options. The Options dialog box appears.

2. Click the Sending tab (see Figure 23.2).

FIGURE 23.2 Set options for sending mail.

3. In the When Composing New Messages area, click the Font button to choose a different font for message text.

4. Under Tracking Options, choose when you want to be notified about mail you've sent.

5. In Save Copies of Messages in "Sent Items" Folder, choose the options you want to use for saving messages.

6. When you're done, click Apply to save the changes and view another tab, or click OK to save the changes and close the dialog box.

Reading Options   Take a look at the Reading tab in the
Options dialog box. It contains options you can use to
choose fonts for message replies that you send and for
forwarded messages.

SETTING CALENDAR OPTIONS

If you work during unusual days or hours, you can change your
default Calendar work week in the Calendar tab of the Options
dialog box. Suppose your work week runs from Tuesday through
Saturday, and your work day is from 4 am to 12 noon. You can
make changes to the Calendar so that it reflects your actual work
week. You can also set your time zone and add holidays to your
calendar.

To set Calendar options, follow these steps:

1. Choose Tools, Options. The Options dialog box appears.

2. Click the Calendar tab (see Figure 23.3).

3. In the Calendar Work Week area, choose the days of the
   week you usually work (the default is Monday through
   Friday). You also can set the first day of your week and
   the first week of your year.

4. In the Calendar Working Hours area, set your starting and
   ending time (the default is 8 am to 5 pm).

5. To set the time zone for your area, click the Time Zone
   button, and then choose the zone that describes your
   location.

6. To add holidays to your calendar, click the Add Holidays
   button. Then check the box representing your country
   (US is default) and click OK. Outlook imports the US holidays to the calendar.

7. When you're done, click Apply to save the changes and
   view another tab, or click OK to save the changes and
   close the dialog box.

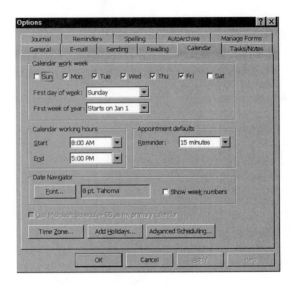

FIGURE 23.3 Set your calendar work week to suit your schedule.

In this lesson, you learned to set e-mail, calendar, and other options in Outlook. In the next lesson, you learn to use Internet services.

USING INTERNET SERVICES

In this lesson, you learn to create an Internet e-mail address, connect to the Internet, and get your Internet e-mail.

SETTING UP AN INTERNET PROFILE

There are many ways you can send messages in Outlook; the LAN (Local Area Network) is the most common method. You must add an Internet user profile to information services. To complete this task, you'll need to obtain information from your Internet service provider (ISP) on the host, your domain, account name and password, and so on.

ISP (Internet Service Provider) A commercial, educational, or government institution, for example, that provides individuals and companies access to the Internet.

POP3 (Post Office Protocol version 3) A set of rules used to download mail to your computer. Your ISP uses a POP3 host, or server, to get your mail to you.

SMTP (Simple Mail Transfer Protocol) A set of rules used to transfer Internet mail. Your ISP goes through an SMTP host, or relay, server to get your mail to you.

To set up an Internet Mail information service, follow these steps:

1. In the Inbox, choose Tools, Services. The Services dialog box appears, with the Services tab displayed.

2. Click the Add button, and the Add Service to Profile dialog box appears (see Figure 24.1).

Figure 24.1   Add the Internet service to your user profile.

3. Select Internet Mail from the Available Information Services list.

4. Click OK, and the Internet Mail dialog box appears. Enter the following information:

> Full Name   Your name should appear in the text box; if not, enter it.

> E-Mail Address   Enter your address from your Internet account (such as splumley@wvvaa.com).

> Internet Mail Server   From your Internet Service Provider (ISP), enter the name or IP address of the mail server running the POP3. This address may be in number format (11.116.55.68) or in words (wvvaa.com).

> Account Name   From your ISP, enter your POP3 e-mail account name.

> Password   From your ISP, enter your password.

5. Choose the Advanced Options dialog box if your ISP uses an SMTP host that is different from the POP3. In the dialog box, enter the name or number of your SMTP host and choose OK.

To set up the connection for Internet mail, follow these steps:

1. Click the Connection tab in the Internet Mail dialog box and choose one of the following options:

Connect Using the Network   Connects to the Internet using a network (LAN) connection.

Connect Using a Modem   Connects to the Internet using a modem.

 TIP **Dial-Up Networking Must Be Installed**   To use the modem connection to the Internet, you must have installed Dial-Up Networking with Windows 95 Setup. If you have not installed Dial-Up Networking, use Add/Remove Programs in the Control Panel to add it. If you're not sure if it's installed, open the My Computer window and see if the Dial-Up Networking folder is there.

2. If you chose to use the modem, you must enter your ISP's designated Internet phone number in the Dial Using the Following Connection text box. Click the Add Entry button to add the number. Then follow the directions on-screen.

3. After adding the entry, Outlook returns to the Internet Mail dialog box. In the Connection tab, click the Edit Entry button. The Properties dialog box for the connection appears.

4. Enter the telephone number, the area code, and the country code (if applicable).

5. Choose the modem type and click the Configure button if you need to check your modem settings.

6. Click the Server Type, and the Server Types dialog box appears. Enter the options as dictated by your ISP.

7. You must configure TCP/IP before you can access the Internet. Click the TCP/IP Settings button, and the TCP/IP dialog box appears.

8. Enter the IP address and domain name server's addresses; if you're unsure, cleck with your ISP.

9. Click OK for each dialg box that's open. You must exit Outlook, log off, and then restart the program for the changes to take effect.

You must also make sure you've installed TCP/IP protocol to your computer. In the Control Panel, open the Networking option. In the Services tab, check the list for TCP/IP protocol; if it isn't there, click the Add button, add and confgure the TCP/IP protocol, and close the dialog box. You'll have to restart the computer for the changes to take effect.

ADDING AN INTERNET E-MAIL ADDRESS

You can send e-mail messages to the Net from the Inbox in Outlook. You can enter the Internet address in a new message, in your address book, or in your Contacts list.

To enter an Internet e-mail address in a new message, simply type the address in the To text box. To enter the address in your address book, choose Tools, Address Book. (See Lesson 7, "Using the Address Book," for more information.)

To enter an Internet e-mail address, follow these steps:

1. Open the Contacts folder, and create a new contact or open an existing one.

2. Enter the Internet e-mail address in the E-Mail text box.

3. If you want, enter a second address in the E-Mail 2 text box.

Internet E-Mail Address   An address that contains a user name and a domain name, separated by an "at" sign (@). Take, for example, the e-mail address splumley@wvvaa.com. In this address, splumley is the user name, and wvvaa.com is the domain name. The com part of the address is the domain name extension, which indicates the domain type (com represents a commercial institution).

USING INTERNET MAIL

Most likely, you use Outlook over a LAN connection or a remote access connection (using a modem to access the server). When you add the Internet information service to your user profile, you can specify that Outlook check one or all services for new mail. To do so, choose Tools, Check for New Mail On and select the appropriate text boxes for the services you want to check, including the Internet. Checking multiple check boxes ensures that Outlook will get your mail from all sources.

To send mail over the Internet, create the message and click the Send button. Make sure you're using an appropriate Internet e-mail address.

Outlook dials the ISP's number you specify and displays a Connecting To dialog box as it accesses your ISP. You can click the Cancel button in this dialog box if you change your mind.

Outlook checks for messages and displays the Deliver Messages dialog box, informing you that it is sending messages and receiving messages. You also can cancel this dialog box by clicking the Cancel button.

As the connection continues, Outlook downloads your mail messages and sends any messages with Internet e-mail addresses. Figure 24.2 displays the Inbox screen after messages are collected from the Internet.

Drag this line to widen a column.

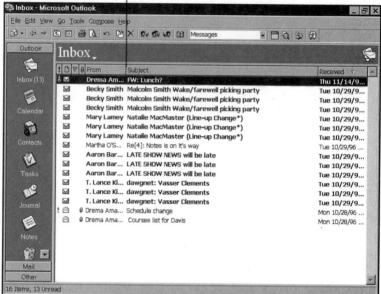

FIGURE 24.2   Read and answer Internet e-mail as you would any other.

In this lesson, you learned to enter an Internet e-mail address, connect to the Internet, and get your Internet e-mail.

WINDOWS 95 AND WINDOWS NT PRIMER

Windows 95 and Windows NT are graphical operating systems that make your computer easy to use by providing menus and pictures from which you select. Before you can take advantage of either operating system, however, you need to learn some basics that apply to both of them.

Fortunately, Windows 95 and Windows NT operate very much alike. (In fact, they're so similar I'll refer to them both just as Windows throughout the remainder of this appendix.) If the figures you see in this primer don't look exactly like what's on your screen, don't sweat it. Some slight variation may occur depending on your setup, the applications you use, and whether you're on a network. Rest assured, however, that the basic information presented here applies no matter what your setup may be.

A FIRST LOOK AT WINDOWS

You don't really have to start Windows because it starts automatically when you turn on your PC. After the initial startup screens, you arrive at a screen something like the one shown in Figure A.1.

PARTS OF THE SCREEN

As you can see, the Windows screen contains a lot of special elements and controls. Here's a brief summary of those elements:

- The Desktop consists of the background and icons that represent programs, tools, and other elements.

- The Taskbar shows a button for each open window and program. You can switch between open windows and programs by clicking the taskbar button that represents the program you want. (The program you are currently working in is highlighted in the taskbar.)

Icons   Start button   Mouse pointer   Buttons for open programs   Taskbar   Desktop

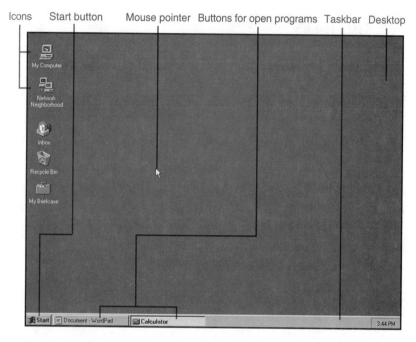

Figure A.1   The Windows screen.

- The Start button opens a menu from which you can start programs, get help, and find files. To use it, you click the Start button, and then you point or click to make a selection from each successive menu that appears. (When you point to a selection that has a right-pointing arrow beside it, a secondary—or cascading—menu appears.)

- The icons that appear on your desktop give you access to certain programs and computer components. You open an icon by double-clicking it. (An open icon displays a window containing programs, files, or other items.)

- The mouse pointer moves around the screen in relation to your movement of the mouse. You use the mouse pointer to select what you want to work with.

You'll learn more about these elements as you work through the rest of this Windows primer.

Also Appearing: Microsoft Office   If your computer has Microsoft Office installed on it, the Office Shortcuts toolbar also appears on-screen. It's a series of little pictures strung together horizontally that represent Office programs. Hold the mouse over a picture (icon) to see what it does; click it to launch the program. See your Microsoft Office documentation to learn more.

You may have some other icons on your desktop (representing networks, folders, printers, files, and so on) depending upon what options you chose during initial setup. Double-click an icon to view the items it contains.

USING A MOUSE

To work most efficiently in Windows, you need a mouse. You will perform the following mouse actions as you work:

- **Point**   To position the mouse so that the on-screen pointer touches an item.

- **Click**   To press and release the left mouse button once. Clicking an item usually selects it. Except when you're told to do otherwise (i.e., to right-click), you always use the left mouse button.

Southpaw Strategy   You can reverse these mouse button actions if you want to use the mouse left-handed. To do so, click Start, Settings, Control Panel, and Mouse. Then click the Buttons tab of the Control Panel dialog box and choose Left-handed.

- **Double-click**   To press and release the left mouse button twice quickly. Double-clicking usually activates an item or opens a window, folder, or program. (Double-clicking may take some practice because the speed needs to be just right. To change the speed so it better matches your "clicking style," choose Start, Settings, Control Panel, and Mouse. Then click the Buttons tab of the Mouse Properties dialog box and adjust the double-clicking speed so that it's just right for you.

- **Drag**   To place the mouse pointer over the element you want to move, press and hold down the left mouse button, and then move the mouse to a new location. You might drag to move a window, dialog box, or file from one location to another. Except when you're told to do otherwise (i.e., to right-drag), you drag with the left mouse button.

- **Right-click**   To click with the right mouse button. Right-clicking usually displays a shortcut (or pop-up) menu from which you can choose common commands.

Controlling a Window with the Mouse

Ever wonder why the program is called "Windows"? Well, Windows operating systems section off the desktop into rectangular work areas called "windows." These windows are used for particular purposes, such as running a program, displaying options or lists, and so on. Each window has common features used to manipulate the window. Figure A.2 shows how you can use the mouse to control your windows.

TIP   **Scrolling for Information**   If your window contains more information than it can display at once, scroll bars appear on the bottom and/or right edges of the window. To move through the window's contents, click an arrow button at either end of a scroll bar to move in that direction, or drag the scroll box in the direction you want to move.

If you're using the professional version of Office 97, you'll also have enhanced scrolling available to you via your "Intellimouse"—a new mouse by Microsoft that includes a scrolling wheel. Using this mouse is described in all Que books that cover Microsoft Office 97 and its individual applications.

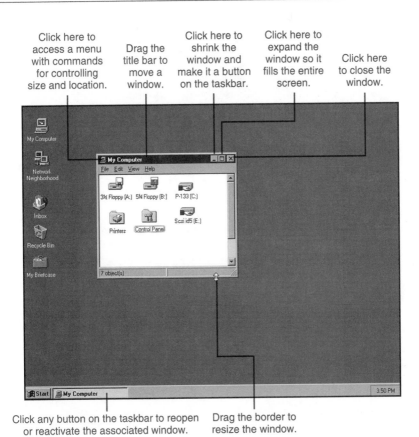

Click here to access a menu with commands for controlling size and location.

Drag the title bar to move a window.

Click here to shrink the window and make it a button on the taskbar.

Click here to expand the window so it fills the entire screen.

Click here to close the window.

Click any button on the taskbar to reopen or reactivate the associated window.

Drag the border to resize the window.

FIGURE A.2   Use your mouse to control and manipulate windows.

USING MENUS

Almost every Windows program has a menu bar that contains menus. The menu names appear in a row across the top of the screen. To open a menu, click its name (after you click anywhere in the menu bar, you need only point to a menu name to produce the drop-down menu). The menu drops down, displaying its commands (as shown in Figure A.3). To select a command, you simply click it.

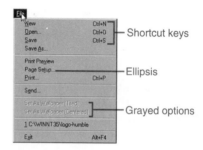

FIGURE A.3   A menu lists various commands you can perform.

Usually, when you select a command, Windows executes the command immediately. But you need to keep the following exceptions to that rule in mind:

- If the command name is gray (instead of black), the command is unavailable at the moment, and you cannot choose it.

- If the command name is followed by an arrow (as the selections on the Start menu are), selecting the command causes another menu to appear, from which you must make another selection.

- If the command is followed by an ellipsis (...), selecting it will cause a dialog box to appear. You'll learn about dialog boxes later in this primer.

TIP

Shortcut Keys   Key names appear after some command names (for example, Ctrl+O appears to the right of the Open command, and Ctrl+S appears next to the Save command). These are shortcut keys, and you can use them to perform the command without opening the menu. You should also note that some menu names and commands have one letter underlined. By pressing Alt+the underlined letter in a menu name, you can open the menu; by pressing the underlined letter in a command name, you can select that command from the open menu.

Using Shortcut Menus

A fairly new feature in Windows is the shortcut or pop-up menu. Right-click any object (any icon, screen element, file, or folder), and a shortcut menu like the one shown in Figure A.4 appears. The shortcut menu contains commands that apply only to the selected object. Click any command to select it, or click outside the menu to cancel it.

Navigating Dialog Boxes

A dialog box is Windows way of requesting additional information or giving you information. For example, if you choose Print from the File menu of the WordPad application, you see a dialog box something like the one shown in Figure A.5. (The options it displays will vary from system to system.)

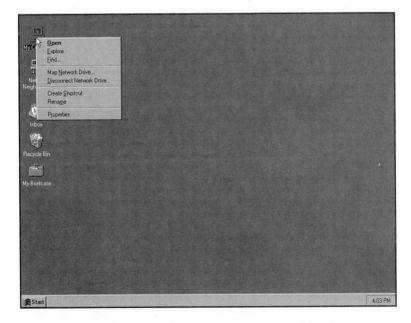

Figure A.4   Shortcut menus are new in Windows 95 and Windows NT 4.0.

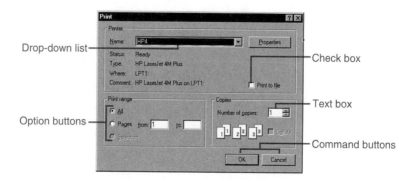

Figure A.5   A dialog box often requests additional information.

Each dialog box contains one or more of the following elements:

- List boxes display available choices. Click any item in the list to select it. If the entire list is not visible, use the scroll bar to see additional choices.

- Drop-down lists are similar to list boxes, but only one item in the list is shown. To see the rest of the list, click the drop-down arrow (to the right of the list box), and then click an item to select it.

- Text boxes allow you to type an entry. Just click inside the text box and type. Text boxes that are designed to hold numbers usually have up and down arrow buttons (called increment buttons) that let you bump the number up and down.

- Check boxes enable you to turn individual options on or off by clicking them. (A check mark or "X" appears when an option is on.) Each check box is an independent unit that doesn't affect other check boxes.

- Option buttons are like check boxes, except that option buttons appear in groups and you can select only one. When you select an option button, the program automatically deselects whichever one was previously selected. Click a button to activate it, and a black bullet appears inside of the white option circle.

- Command buttons perform an action, such as executing the options you set (OK), canceling the options (Cancel), closing the dialog box, or opening another dialog box. To select a command button, click it.

- Tabs bring up additional "pages" of options you can choose. Click a tab to activate it.

FROM HERE

If you need more help with Windows, you may want to pick up one of these books:

The Complete Idiot's Guide to Windows 95 by Paul McFedries

Easy Windows 95 by Sue Plumley

The Big Basics Book of Windows 95 by Shelley O'Hara, Jennifer Fulton, and Ed Guilford

Using Windows 95 by Ed Bott

The Complete Idiot's Guide to Windows NT 4.0 Workstation by Paul McFedries

Using Windows NT 4.0 Workstation by Ed Bott

D

E